Real Stories of Big Cat Rescues

Melanie Bowlin

With contributions by
Audra Masternak

Photographs by
Stephen D. McCloud

Foreword by
Camilla Calamandrei

QUARRY BOOKS

an imprint of
INDIANA UNIVERSITY PRESS
BLOOMINGTON AND INDIANAPOLIS

Real Stories of
BIG
CAT
RESCUES

Tales from the Exotic Feline Rescue Center

This book is a publication of

Quarry Books
an imprint of

Indiana University Press
601 North Morton Street
Bloomington, Indiana 47404-3797 USA

www.iupress.indiana.edu

Telephone orders   800-842-6796
Fax orders   812-855-7931
Orders by e-mail   iuporder@indiana.edu

This book is printed on acid-free paper.

Manufactured in China

Library of Congress Cataloging-in-Publication Data

Bowlin, Melanie.
  Real stories of big cat rescues : tales from the
Exotic Feline Rescue Center / Melanie Bowlin ; with
contributions by Audra Masternak ; photographs by
Stephen D. McCloud ; foreword by Camilla Calamandrei.
     p. cm.
  ISBN 978-0-253-22234-3 (pbk. : alk. paper) 1. Felidae—
Indiana—Center Point. 2. Exotic Feline Rescue Center
(Center Point, Ind.) 3. Wildlife rescue—Indiana—Center Point.
4. Animal sanctuaries—Indiana—Center Point.
I. Masternak, Audra. II. Title.
  QL737.C23B694 2010
  639.97'97550977244—dc22
                                        2010005756

1 2 3 4 5 15 14 13 12 11 10

REAL STORIES OF BIG CAT RESCUES
is dedicated to the hard-working EFRC staff,
especially head keeper Rebecca Rizzo

May the time come when all men will recognize the fact that the laws of God and humanity require us to be merciful to the dumb animals, and to grant the same justice and mercy to them we would ask for ourselves.

Indiana author Gene Stratton-Porter,
Strike at Shane's

Contents

Foreword

During the winter of 2003, I started researching a documentary film about captive-bred tigers in the United States. At the beginning, I thought I was researching a couple of unique and bizarre stories of people who wanted to keep big cats as pets. Over the six years that I worked on the film, which is now known as "The Tiger Next Door," it became clear that I was telling the story of a nationwide crisis of wild-animal keeping.

My foray into this world started when I first read about a woman in New Jersey named Joan Byron-Marasek. In January 1999 a 400 lb. adult tiger was found wandering through Monmouth County, New Jersey. The tiger was seen in a variety of places over the course of the day. It eventually made the mistake of trespassing onto the property of a new housing development (coincidentally called "The Preserve") where homeowners were, reasonably, much alarmed. After various attempts to approach the tiger, local police decided that they could not effectively tranquilize the animal, so they shot the cat dead.

Where did that tiger come from?

Some speculated that the tiger could have escaped from the nearby Six Flags Adventure Park. Others suggested that it might have escaped from a private tiger owner in the area. One neighborhood resident later told me they thought there was a local garage band that had been keeping a tiger as its mascot. Officials, however, suspected that the tiger came from a local tiger sanctuary known as Tigers Only Preservation Society (T.O.P.S.)—which was owned and operated by Joan Byron-Marasek. Although it was never proven that the tiger came from her property, the incident led to an inspection of T.O.P.S. that revealed a facility in great disrepair, serving as home to 24 adult tigers. Most of the tigers were living in cages with several inches of mud, feces, and urine. There were no pools of water for the animals to play in, or toys for stimulation. A large male was kept in a trailer with only one small window. It was a sad and squalid situation.

Amazingly, Byron-Marasek's backyard facility was actually licensed by the United States Department of Agriculture (USDA). She had been granted a license for exhibiting tigers several years earlier, but there was no record that she ever did exhibit them. Byron-Marasek's operation was also sanctioned by the state of New Jersey, which granted her a permit to keep tigers for educational purposes. However, there was no record that she had ever held any educational programs with her animals. Both of these organizations—the USDA and the state of New Jersey—had been (theoretically) inspecting the T.O.P.S. compound regularly, checking for appropriate safety, cleanliness, and animal husbandry.

Based on the appalling conditions found in 1999, the state of New Jersey made preparations to confiscate the tigers and move them. It was challenging to find a sanctuary that could take all 24 animals. Fortunately, a sanctuary in Texas agreed to take most of them—if the state of New Jersey would finance the move and contribute to the cost of the new caging needed. (Total cost: $144,555.)

Byron-Marasek took the state of New Jersey to court to stop the move. She lost, but went on to appeal several times over the next three years. Finally, by late 2002 (almost four years after the tiger escape) it seemed that the state of New Jersey had prevailed. Byron-Marasek's tigers would be confiscated and moved to Texas, as soon as possible.

As a filmmaker and animal lover, I was intrigued by the story. It seemed so surprising and unique. Little did I know I could have picked any month of the year and found a big cat "rescue" happening someplace in the United States. The sanctuary where Byron-Marasek's tigers would end up already had almost 600 captive-bred animals. This included tigers, lions, ligers (cross-bred tiger and lion), cougars, lynx, ocelots, servals, bears, chimps, and other kinds of big cats and monkeys. The director of the sanctuary patiently explained to me that each of these animals was captive bred and almost all came from private owners—or in the case of the monkeys, medical research labs. It was hard for me to appreciate the scope of what I was seeing and comprehend what it meant that one sanctuary could have so many animals and be getting calls to take in more every day. Soon, though, a series of shocking events would startle me into a deeper understanding of the crisis at hand.

It was October 3, 2003. I was busy lining up crew and making preparations to film the transfer of the New Jersey tigers, which was scheduled for early November. The news came that Roy Horn (of famed performance duo Seigfried and Roy) had been attacked by one of his own tigers while performing on stage in Las Vegas. The 7-year-old tiger, known as Montecore, had been captive bred and had been performing in front of the public since he was 6 months old. The incident seemed both inevitable and impossible. Roy Horn was considered one of the top tiger handlers in the world. As many would say afterwards—if it could happen to him, it could happen to anyone. The very next day (October 4), a full-grown, 2-year-old tiger named Ming was found in an apartment in Harlem, New York. The owner had bought the tiger from a breeder as a cub and had secretly raised him in the apartment. In order to relocate the 425 lb. tiger, an officer had to rappel down the outside of the building to shoot the tiger with a tranquilizer through the window. Later, a caiman (a reptile that resembles a crocodile) was also found in the apartment. The owner told reporters he was trying to reproduce the Garden of Eden.

Were these animals everywhere? Could anyone get one? I finally understood that the New Jersey tigers that were moved to Texas on November 12 were only the tip of the iceberg—evidence of a much larger, nationwide crisis of wild-animal keeping.

On December 14 of the same year, it was reported that a woman's pet tiger in Miller's Creek, North Carolina, had killed her 10-year-old nephew. The tiger had been kept in a cage in the backyard. The newspapers said that the tiger pulled the boy under the wall of his cage, where the family dog had dug a hole, and mauled the boy to death. Five weeks later (January 25, 2004), just 50 miles from the previous incident, another pet tiger attacked a 14-year-old girl. The girl's family lived in a trailer and they, too, kept the tiger in a cage in their backyard.

There were then, and are still, thousands of these large wild animals being kept in private captivity around the country. And by private captivity I mean backyards, basements, attics, barns, and cages by the side of the road—called "roadside zoos." All over the United States people are keeping tigers, cougars, leopards, and other big cats. Some have one or two. Others have ten or twenty, or collections that include bears, wolves, and other large wild animals.

Tigers, unfortunately for them, are particularly plentiful in these situations because they breed very well in captivity. As a result, even an untrained individual can easily breed for cubs and many do. Although every tiger owner I met while making my film had gone bankrupt at least once while keeping these animals, they all thought they could make a profit off the animals somehow. Or at least make enough to cover the expenses of keeping the animals. The most common idea seems to be to use tiger cubs for photo "ops" ("get your picture taken with this baby tiger for $12," for example) or "educational" appearances at schools. But that can only last for a few months. Soon the cub is too big to be used safely and legally for these activities. An owner might then decide to breed the tiger with another tiger (someone else's that they borrow or share) so they can have a litter of cubs. The owners of the tigers will split each litter, keeping some cubs and selling others—in most cases to other private owners. Over the years, this ever-increasing circle of backyard tiger breeders has led to a massive overpopulation of captive-bred tigers, to the point that there are more tigers in the United States than there are appropriate places to keep them. Sanctuaries like the Exotic Feline Rescue Center turn down cats looking for homes every day. In fact, experts like Ron Tilson of the Minneapolis Zoo agree that now there are most likely more captive-bred tigers in the U.S. than are roaming wild in the world.

So what does a person do with an adult tiger (or lion, or cougar) when they decide they don't want it anymore? As Joe Taft of the Exotic Feline Rescue Center explains: "The zoos don't want them, and we can't take any more animals. So even if you want to surrender a big cat or bear, you can't." Animals that might have once sold for thousands of dollars are today being given away, ultimately ending up who knows where.

At the same time that the market for live adult tigers has collapsed, demand for tiger hide, tiger bone, tiger meat, and other body parts is still strong—especially in Asia. As a result, captive-bred tigers in the U.S. (and Asia) are now worth more dead than alive. Special Agent Tim Santel of U.S. Fish and Wildlife learned this firsthand when he led an undercover investigation out of his office in Illinois that exposed a ring of men in the Midwest collecting "unwanted tiger pets." The men would kill the tigers and sell their hides, teeth, skulls, tails, meat, and so forth, ultimately making well over $1,000 per tiger. Santel says: "This whole cat craze is really being driven by money. I don't want to paint everybody with a broad brush, but, in the end, the reason people are breeding and buying and selling is money."

The international watchdog group called TRAFFIC, which monitors trade in wildlife around the world, published a paper in 2008 speculating that there may indeed be a growing black market of tiger parts in the United States: tiger parts that are being sold in the U.S. and also in Asia. (Tiger conservationists are concerned that increased availability of tiger parts actually fuels—rather than quenches—demand and increases the poaching threat to the 3,000–5,000 tigers surviving in the wild.)

So what now? While conservation organizations around the world are working to protect habitats for the surviving tigers in the wild, other organizations have been working closer to home. Groups like Born Free and the Humane Society of the United States have been working steadfastly for many years now to introduce legislation state by state, with the hope that each state will ban ownership of wild animals as pets. They are making progress. When the tiger escaped in New Jersey in 1999 there were only 13 states with regulations restricting ownership of tigers and other large wild animals. Now there are 29 states with some kind of ban or partial ban on keeping tigers as pets. Additionally, the U.S. Congress passed the Captive Wildlife Safety Act in 2003 (effective 2007) which makes it illegal for a private individual to purchase a wild animal in a state where wild animals auctions are legal, and drive that animal home across state lines. (USDA license holders are exempt.)

Unfortunately, this sounds a bit better than it is. As this book goes to press, there are still 21 states in which it is legal to own a tiger or other large wild animal as a pet. (In 12 of these states you need a permit; in 9 states no license of any kind is required.) And in the states with a ban on wild animal pet ownership, many private owners are able to keep their animals by getting a federal license from the USDA. The USDA issues class A licenses for breeders of large wild animals, class B licenses for dealers, and class C licenses for exhibitors. Private owners may claim that they are breeding for conservation or for sale; selling their animals to zoos and performers or for medical research; and/or exhibiting their animals for educational or entertainment purposes—this would include roadside zoos, safari parks, and circuses. This means many private animal collectors and owners of roadside zoos around the country hold the same USDA class C exhibitor license that is held by major conservation zoos such as the Bronx Zoo and the San Diego Zoo.

This mind-bending reality is a function of two things. One is that the existing USDA regulations for keeping animals in a safe and humane way are woefully inadequate. Some might say, inhumane. According to the Animal Welfare Act of the United States, any animal in captivity—including tigers, bears, and lions—is only required to have caging big enough to stand up and turn around in. This is not the standard for transporting an animal. This is the standard for how an animal will live out its entire life. The Animal Welfare Act also requires that captive animals have shelter of some kind from the weather, have access to food and water, and have a cage that is kept free of filth and clutter.

The other reason that terrible facilities and decent facilities often end up with the same class of USDA licenses is that the section of the USDA responsible for overseeing captive wild animals is severely understaffed. USDA agents are not able to visit facilities regularly and when they find violations they are inconsistent about following up. This shocking lack of oversight and enforcement is what has allowed for cases like the one involving the 24 tigers in New Jersey, and the even more horrifying case involving a man named John Weinhart in Riverside, California. Weinhart was a longtime tiger "rescuer" (he claims to have been doing it for more than 35 years) and ran a USDA-licensed sanctuary called Tiger Rescue for retired animal actors. In April 2003, U.S. Fish and Wildlife officers were tipped off that Weinhart was keeping unlicensed wild animals at his home. When they raided his house, they found a litter of newborn tiger cubs and leopard cubs in the attic, and two juvenile tigers on the property. They also found the remains of more than 80 dead tigers, including a truck full of air-dried tiger pelts, a freezer full of frozen tiger cubs, and miscellaneous decomposing animal corpses. John Weinhart's 8-year-old son lived with him at this property.

Five months earlier officials had seized ten tigers from Tiger Rescue and cited Weinhart with serious animal welfare violations, but the facility was still up and running. (As of 2009, under the Obama administration, USDA now posts inspection reports online for the public to see.) When authorities returned to the sanctuary, after the raid on Weinhart's house, they found 54 big cats (such as lions, tigers, leopards) without food or water. (Eight of the leopards from Tiger Rescue would eventually find refuge at the Exotic Feline Rescue Center.)

What does it say about us as a nation that we allow this to happen? Why isn't the USDA held responsible when they repeatedly fail to prevent or anticipate violations and animal cruelty of this scale? If it were a private organization wouldn't it be out of business by now, and paying off fines for its failings? And why are thousands of tigers, lions, cougars, bears, and other animals in these situations to begin with? Do we believe, as a nation, that animals that naturally roam hundreds of miles should be condemned to life in a cage, because someone thinks it would be nice to have one as a pet, or profitable to keep one as part of a roadside zoo?

Many tiger owners will tell you that if we don't keep these animals alive in captivity then they will become extinct, because they cannot survive in the wild any longer. And that is true. We are destroying the natural habitat of the tiger, and that of other large wild animals around the world. But if we are going to keep some of these animals alive in captivity for our own pleasure, then surely we can find a small group of highly qualified, ethical professionals to breed them appropriately for species preservation; actively limit the number of animals subjected to life in captivity; and provide those that are in captivity an appropriate quality of life.

Camilla Calamandrei
Sleepy Hollow, New York

Unloading a new arrival

Joe and Velda, September 21, 2008 (above), and
Jean with Max and Kisa, July 8, 2006 (below)

Preface

More than four years have passed since *Saving the Big Cats* was published. During this time the abuse of animals in the United States has continued to increase and the number of felids at the Exotic Feline Rescue Center (EFRC) has grown to almost two hundred. Politicians and the general public have shown little interest in solving the problem of animal neglect. EFRC constantly receives calls about animals in need of a home, as do zoos and other rescue facilities. The need for EFRC and other facilities like it thus seems apparent. Everything described in the foreword to the first book is still true today. Some things never change.

Some changes, however, have been made at the Center to accommodate the large number of cats it provides a home for. Much to the relief of most visitors, butchering is no longer done at the main entrance. A large building with $45,000 worth of refrigeration was added to the Center, and so butchering now takes place indoors and out of view. Staff now use vehicles for hauling meat to the enclosures instead of wheelbarrows. Breaking apart frozen chicken outdoors in twenty-degree weather is a memory many of us would like to forget. And EFRC director Joe Taft rides in a golf cart instead of walking or riding a bicycle over the 109 acres. Jean Herrberg, assistant director, no longer works with the feeding crew. Her time is spent on fundraisers, educational talks, and paperwork. Our wish list remains long. Income remains short.

Felids have relatively short lifetimes—fifteen to twenty years in captivity—and so it's not surprising that some animals have died and new ones have taken their place since the first book was published. Zavata, Bobette, Coco, Menelik, Prince, Princess, Princie, Otis, Majae, Bobbie Sue, BC, Molly, Charlie, Kashka, Olaf, Lilly, Cody, Ben, and others are dearly missed. They were family and friends to many of the people at EFRC.

Stephen D. McCloud

Preface

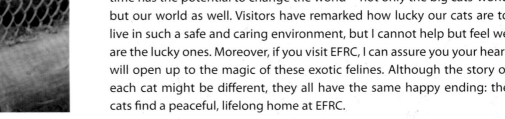

After reading a 2005 newspaper article about EFRC, located in Center Point, Indiana, I decided to make the drive from Indianapolis. I could not have known how that trip would change my life. The article did not prepare me for the magic of this animal haven. Most people no doubt assume that if they want to see a lion or tiger in the United States, they will have to go to a zoo, where the animals are enclosed in structures made of concrete and metal. But visitors to the Center see grass, trees, and wild vegetation at every turn. To be able to encounter these beautiful animals in such a natural environment is a gift for all.

This is why I became a volunteer tour guide. Despite my full-time teaching job, everyday responsibilities, and the one-hour commute to EFRC, I felt compelled to do my small part to contribute to this wonderful organization. Guiding tours has allowed me to share the history of these great cats and educate our visitors about exotic felines' needs. While volunteering I have met people from all over the United States as well as the world. To see visitors' eyes grow wide when they hear a lion roar for the first time is an amazing sight, no matter how many times you've seen it. Never did they think a six-hundred-pound tiger would greet them with a friendly chuff or that they would hear a puma purr. These are just a few of the wonderful experiences people have when they visit.

What an honor it is to be in the presence of such powerful yet graceful animals. I would like to thank Joe Taft and Jean Herrberg for allowing me to play a role, small as it is, in saving these big cats. Saving one cat at a time has the potential to change the world—not only the big cats' world but our world as well. Visitors have remarked how lucky our cats are to live in such a safe and caring environment, but I cannot help but feel we are the lucky ones. Moreover, if you visit EFRC, I can assure you your heart will open up to the magic of these exotic felines. Although the story of each cat might be different, they all have the same happy ending: the cats find a peaceful, lifelong home at EFRC.

Melanie Bowlin

Melanie, May 17, 2008

Acknowledgments

I could not have attempted or completed this project without the help of family and friends. I would like to thank my critique group—Lori Antony, Carol Bowlin, Lisa DeVault, Ann Hedderick, and Darla Rampersaud. I would also like to express my thanks to Stephen McCloud for saying the words that gave me the opportunity to do this book—"I'll do a new book if you'll write it." Those words fulfilled my lifelong dream of becoming a published author. I would also like to thank all fellow volunteers at EFRC for their hard work and dedication to the over two hundred big cats at EFRC.

Melanie Bowlin

Real Stories of Big Cat Rescues

THE ORIGINS OF EFRC

Joe Taft was twenty years old when he walked into a pet shop in Terre Haute, Indiana, and bought an ocelot. Although today Joe strongly disapproves of exotic pet ownership, his fantasy at the time was to drive around fast in a Lotus with a cheetah in the seat beside him. He settled for an MG and an ocelot.

After college, Joe moved onto six acres in New Mexico. At that time, he acquired a one-year-old female leopard. Taaka, as he named her, lived with him as a house pet. She had access to a large outdoor area and the run of the house for nearly nineteen years. Shortly after Taaka's death, Joe bought a thirteen-day-old leopard he named Kiki.

When Kiki was about six months old, Joe happened across a couple of badly abused tigers, BC and Molly. This was his first experience with the mistreatment of exotic felines, and he was outraged. He rescued the two cats—and thus began the effort behind EFRC.

In 1991, Joe left New Mexico and returned to Indiana with Kiki, Molly, and BC. He looked for a piece of land where he would have no immediate neighbors. The fifteen acres he purchased are now the portion of EFRC that is open to visitors. The nonprofit corporation that was subsequently formed to support the Center purchased another eleven acres. Someone later donated money to purchase eighty-two additional acres on the south side of East Ashboro Road.

As Teddy Roosevelt famously said, "If you build it, they will come"—and come they did. Soon someone called and asked whether Joe could take a lion. Then someone else called, hoping that he could take another unwanted feline. Suddenly there were five lions. Then a puma. Then a bobcat. Then many, many more. All were taken on a permanent basis. When a big cat finds its way to EFRC, it has a home for life.

The question new visitors to EFRC most frequently ask is, "Where do these animals come from?" The answer is that by and large they come from circuses, zoos, breeders, and people who have had them as pets. Sometimes animals arrive singly. Other times they come by the truckload. That was the case in the summer of 2000, when the Center took in a large group of exotic felines from one of the worst facilities ever discovered. On August 21 of that year, EFRC workers traveled to Pittsburgh, Pennsylvania, intending to return with two or three lions, which they hoped to introduce to a group of young lions already living at the Center. When they arrived at the facility, they found neglect and abuse beyond belief. In a dark basement that reeked of feline urine and feces were four cages about five feet by five feet. There were three lions in one cage, three tigers in a second cage, and one tiger each in the other two cages. Seven of the cats were severely malnourished and dehydrated. They apparently had been left to die. They weighed 50 to 80 pounds instead of the 200 to 250 pounds that healthy lions or tigers their age should have weighed. The eighth was closer to normal size but still substantially underweight. Fearing that none of these felines would survive, EFRC workers loaded all of them into a truck and headed for Indiana. It was the first time in a long time that the animals had seen sunlight or breathed fresh air.

Two weeks later, a semi pulled up at EFRC. In it were eight more lions and tigers that had been seized by the U.S. Department of Agriculture (USDA) from the same facility in Pennsylvania. After years of having been cited for violations of the Animal Welfare Act, for which the owner's license was revoked and for which he was fined a total of $32,000 in 1997 and 1998, the facility had finally been closed.

Another tiger that had been rescued in Pennsylvania by the USDA was initially placed at a rescue center in Mississippi. He became extremely aggressive there, injuring his cage mate and human staff, so on September 9 he too was transferred to EFRC. He settled in nicely and has become a favorite of most of the workers. Maybe it's his name—Felix—or maybe it's because of his friendly behavior. He never has an unkind word for anyone. He loves his new life and seems to have completely forgotten the abuse he suffered in the past.

There are many other rescue centers. Few, however, come up to the standards of EFRC. Some visitors come expecting a zoo. When was the last time you saw a blind tiger at a zoo? Or a Canada lynx with a neurological problem? Or a puma with frostbitten ears? Zoos want—and more importantly keep—only "perfect" animals, because they are interested in displaying animals in cages for the benefit of humans. Furthermore, whereas zoos are concerned with species survival, EFRC is concerned with individual survival.

When EFRC was incorporated in 1996, there were only about twenty animals housed at the facility, and all the work was done by volunteers. In 2010, there are almost two hundred exotic felines at EFRC, and a board of directors oversees a budget of more than $300,000. Joe has some full-time employees, but the Center's volunteers still play an essential role.

Jean Herrberg is the assistant director for EFRC. Sometime in the mid-1990s, she started coming to the Center as a volunteer. She arrived just in time to hand-raise two baby lions, Spirit and Parker. After traveling back and forth for a few years between Center Point and Columbus, Indiana, where she was a teacher, Jean decided to retire from teaching and move back to Center Point—her original home—where she still had family. Jean spends her time traveling around the country picking up animals, doing educational programs, answering mail, and raising money for the Center.

After one lion died during minor surgery at the office of a local veterinarian, the EFRC staff started taking animals to the University of Illinois—a two-hundred-mile round-trip. In 2004, a new building was completed at the Center with space for a full hospital. Most surgeries are now performed on the grounds.

When Joe Taft rescued BC and Molly all those years ago, little did he know where his act of kindness would lead. With the help of dedicated staff and volunteers, and the generosity of donors who share Joe's passion for these big cats, EFRC has been able to carry out its mission: to let these special animals live a dignified life, in a permanent home, with the best of care.

Stephen D. McCloud

Alex, a male bobcat, came to EFRC via New York accompanied by Shiloh (see "Shiloh," this volume) in December 2007. A retired couple had purchased Alex as a kitten. As they traveled in their motor home, they quickly realized they could not deal with Alex's rapidly increasing size—or his energy level. The couple gave him to a person not licensed to house exotic felines, and the New York State Department of Environmental Conservation subsequently confiscated him.

A medical examination performed on Alex after he arrived at EFRC revealed he was suffering from a flea infestation, from which he was quickly cured. He began his life at EFRC in a small transport cage located in the clinic. Alex was stressed owing to his several relocations, and the quiet clinic environment was free of disturbances that might cause him further anxiety. While he was in temporary housing, construction began on his permanent enclosure—a multilevel structure that provides Alex with the mental and physical stimulation that all bobcats require. The dense vegetation in his enclosure also allows him to take some downtime when visitors are present.

Alex resides with Rocky, a fellow bobcat. Visitors come to their enclosure at the end of the tour. Depending on Alex's mood, you might see him—or you might not.

Alex, January 4, 2009

Alex, April 26, 2009

Alex, March 7, 2008

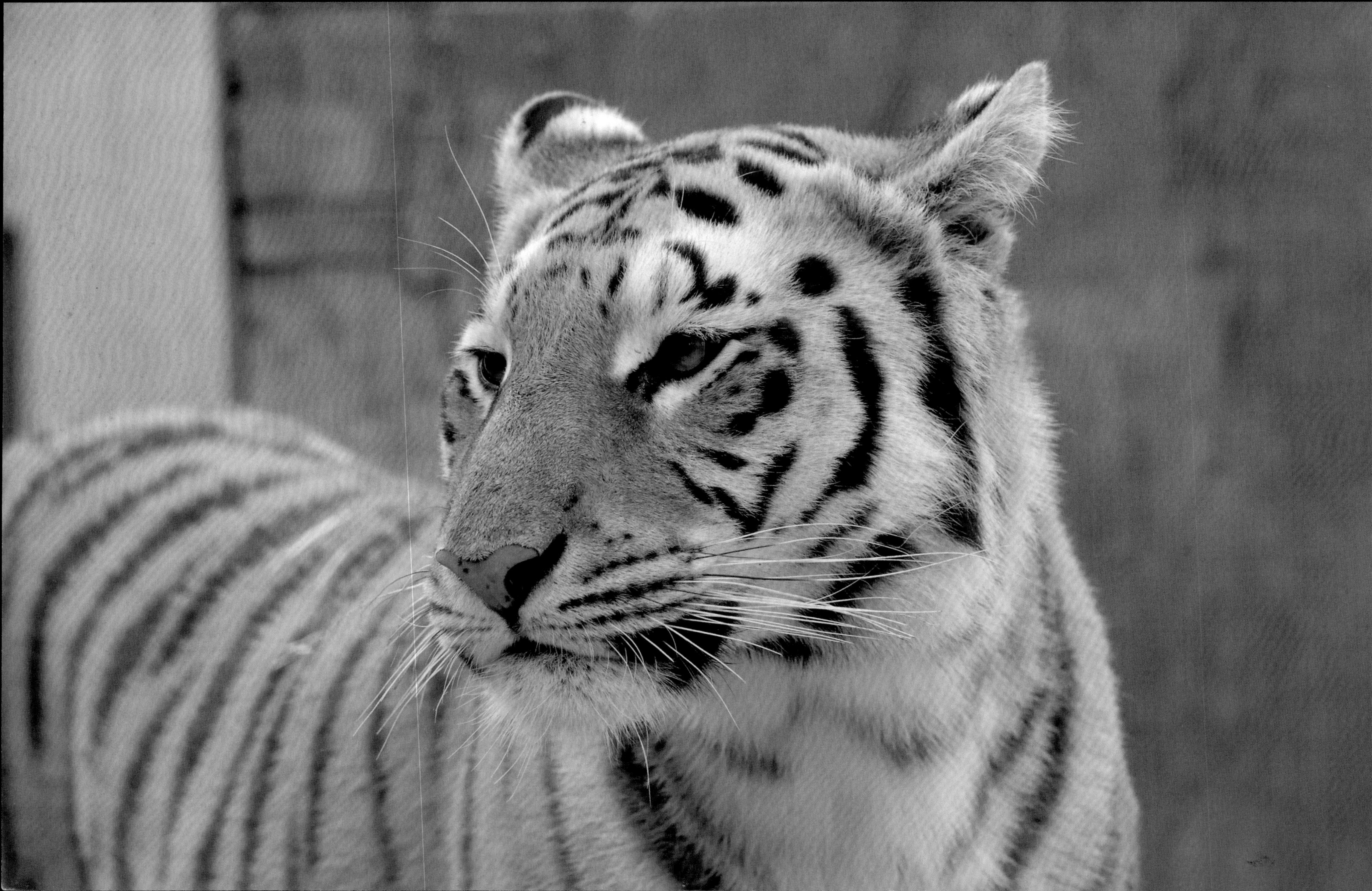

In 2003, when a fifth-grade boy explained to his teacher that his bites and scratches came from a tiger cub, school officials contacted local law enforcement. Arriving at the boy's home, they found Anna, a thirty-five-pound tiger cub. Tiger feces, urine, and raw chicken littered the house. This was not the first time the police had been to the owner's Minnesota home: in 2001, the owner had been convicted of cruelty to animals and prohibited from having any more pets.

Anna was confiscated by the authorities and brought to a veterinarian, who discovered she had sores and scars on her neck (the result of a tight collar), intestinal concerns, borderline anemia, and a dull, dry coat that suggested an inadequate diet.

Anna recovered at the local humane society and then was relocated temporarily to the Wildcat Sanctuary in Sandstone, Minnesota. The Wildcat Sanctuary's director explored the options for little Anna. Because the director had had dealings with EFRC in the past, she contacted the Center and Joe Taft agreed to take the cub and provide her a lifelong home.

Anna is the sweetheart of her enclosure. She loves attention from staff and takes great joy in her three enclosure mates, Herman, Joey, and Sumara. Unfortunately, Anna is not on the public tour.

Anna, August 6, 2006

Anna, October 14, 2007

BABY AND SAM

Lions

In 1993, Baby, an eight-month-old female lion, came to EFRC from Zionsville, Indiana. She moved into an enclosure with a male tiger, Otis Lee. The duo lived peacefully together until Otis Lee's passing in 2008. Although Baby grieved for her enclosure mate, she continued on.

Coincidentally, shortly after Otis Lee's death, EFRC received a call from Baby's breeder in Zionsville regarding a male lion named Sam. Because Sam and Baby had lived with felines in the past, EFRC staff thought it was possible they could room together, which would give them both much-needed companionship.

Little did we realize that the relationship between Baby and Sam would become the talk of EFRC. That Sam and Baby are head over heels in love is apparent to all. Wherever Baby is, Sam is nearby. Visitors will see them lying next to each other, and they will see Sam following behind Baby as she sidles to another location. The most precious sight of all is when Baby and Sam lie down facing one another and put their paws on top of each other.

If visitors catch sight of Baby and Sam during a tour, they will notice Baby's resemblance to a young male lion. Although we have no medical proof, we suspect Baby is going through menopause, or, as one New York visitor cleverly put it, "mane-opause."

Baby and Sam's enclosure is located between the Southern Belles and Maggie.

Baby and Sam, May 3, 2009

Baby, December 17, 2006

Sam, January 23, 2009

Sam, May 3, 2009

Caine, a male tiger, arrived at EFRC on February 8, 1999, along with Sinbad (a black leopard) and Chica (a bobcat). Their Texas owner had left no plans regarding the care of his animals after his death, and so EFRC agreed to house them.

Caine was nine months old when he arrived. Because he was so young, and needed enclosure mates, we decided to house him with five other young tiger cubs: Duke, Eleni, Natasha, Mariah, and Katerina. Caine was the oldest and biggest of the group. Staff remember how adorable Caine appeared when towering over his new feline friends.

Caine still has his people-friendly personality as an adult cat. He saunters to the fence when called and delights in attention from familiar staff. He has also acquired a nickname while at EFRC: "the old man looking for his wallet." The nickname comes from Caine's behavior at feeding time. Instead of coming when called, Caine meanders around his enclosure as if looking for his lost wallet. Staff have no choice but to stand and wait. To the unsuspecting eye, it may look like Caine does not know what to do, but he does. He just does it his way.

Caine's enclosure is located near Lakota and is referred to as Duke's group.

Caine (standing), March 8, 2009

Caine (on left), March 8, 2009

Casey, an eight-year-old tiger, came to EFRC via the New Mexico Department of Game and Fish on July 2, 2001. After being confiscated from a private citizen on May 25, 2001, he temporarily resided at the Rio Grande Zoological Park. He had a few dental problems that were rectified with treatment but otherwise appeared to be a healthy, partially declawed one-year-old tiger cub.

Plans were set in motion to introduce Casey to three young female tigers—Cuddles, Nyla, and Jody—once he got to the Center. When he arrived, he was placed in a small transport cage. Rolling Casey up to the girls' enclosure, we waited anxiously to see their response. Chuffing immediately commenced between the four felines, and so it was obvious they would be friends. Shortly thereafter, staff opened Casey's slide gate, and the three girls ran in to greet him.

Casey's enclosure is located near where the tour starts. The shenanigans of this group provide great joy to visitors and staff. They give grand performances: chasing each other, jumping in and out of their water tanks, leaping up on their climbing towers, and stalking each other—as well as EFRC visitors.

Casey, November 1, 2008

Casey, November 1, 2008

Chopper, weighing in at about seven pounds, is EFRC's only Leopard cat. The convoluted route by which he arrived at EFRC exemplifies what happens to exotic felines who are unlawfully bought and sold in this country. According to the limited information we received, Chopper was born in captivity in the former Yugoslavia and then imported to the United States. When he arrived in Miami, Florida, U.S. customs officials seized him because he lacked the proper CITES (Convention on International Trade in Endangered Species) documentation. He was handed over to the U.S. Fish and Wildlife Service (FWS), where he lingered for one year while the legal process played out. The FWS then contacted EFRC requesting that the Center provide a lifelong home for him. When EFRC agreed, FWS airfreighted Chopper to Indianapolis.

On May 15, 2007, Chopper arrived at EFRC. Initially, Chopper resided in a small transport cage located in the clinic, but he has since moved to his new enclosure behind the director's house. Because Chopper is so very timid and nocturnal by nature, he is not on the public tour. This leaves him plenty of time to explore his multilevel enclosure and also allows him to eat his favorite meal—roadkill squirrels—in private.

Chopper, March 19, 2009

Chopper, June 23, 2007

Watch out! If you are not quick-footed, Felix might welcome you to EFRC with a spray. Although Felix is one of the sweetest cats at EFRC, he is also one of the most notorious sprayers.

Felix lived in an appalling Pennsylvania facility that was shut down in the summer of 2000. (See the story about the Munchkins in Stephen D. McCloud's *Saving the Big Cats* [Indiana University Press, 2006].) EFRC rescued eight cats from this facility, but not Felix, who instead went to a respectable rescue center in Mississippi. Unfortunately, this placement did not go as planned. Felix displayed extremely aggressive behavior. He damaged his cage and posed a safety threat to caretakers and to his cage mate. The director at the Mississippi facility knew EFRC director Joe Taft and asked Joe whether the Center could take Felix in. Joe said yes. Arriving on September 9, 2000, Felix was finally able to begin his journey to becoming the awesome tiger he so deserved to be.

As you approach his enclosure, listen. Do not be surprised if you hear a friendly chuff coming from behind the trees. That is Felix saying hello. Despite his upsetting past, Felix is one of the friendliest cats at EFRC, and—if given the chance—he will tell you all about his adventures.

Felix, May 23, 2009

Felix, March 15, 2008

G. G., a male serval, came to EFRC from a North Carolina facility. This facility rescued several pregnant servals simultaneously and did not have room to keep both the adults and the newborns. When contacted and asked to house a baby, EFRC gladly accepted G. G. He arrived at the Center when he was three weeks old, and there were no words to describe his cuteness. He weighed one pound, five ounces, and was a fuzzy fur ball. Because he was so young, the assistant director had to bottle-feed him a special exotic feline formula every three to four hours. This writer's favorite memory of G. G. is of him being burped by the assistant director. Who knew one had to burp a serval?

As G. G. matured, he grew long ears and longer legs. As is typical with servals, he is not comfortable around most people, but the select few profess G. G. is a delight.

G. G. has a forever home at EFRC, but at this time, he is not on the public tour.

G. G., December 19, 2008 (above), and January 2, 2009 (below)

G. G., December 5, 2008

GABBY I

Lion

Gabby I, a.k.a. Fat Gabby, came to EFRC after a police officer made a routine traffic stop on Interstate 64 and found a three-month-old female lion cub sitting on the front seat of the car. Although initial reports stated that Gabby appeared healthy and displayed no signs of stress, these reports proved untrue. Upon arrival at EFRC, Gabby weighed in at a mere sixteen pounds—half the size of a healthy female lion cub. She also had a broken tail and was suffering from anemia, a heart murmur, and ringworm, but with appropriate medical care, she regained her strength.

Of all the big cats, lions are the least people friendly. At EFRC, Gabby has broken that mold, although she is only friendly with two people, the director and the assistant director.

Gabby has proven to be one of our most photogenic cats. If you peruse Stephen McCloud's website (http://stephendmccloud.wordpress.com/) or the EFRC website (http://www.exoticfelinerescuecenter.org/home.html), you will find pictures of Gabby sitting on Rake (one of her enclosure mates), Gabby biting Rake, and Gabby flirting with Rake. We also like to call Gabby our big old teddy bear. When you stop at her enclosure, look for the lion that could be mistaken for a bear. This is Gabby.

Gabby I, May 27, 2007

Gabby I, January 2, 2009

Gabby I, May 10, 2009

GEORGE AND RODNEY
Leopards

Two spotted leopard brothers arrived at EFRC on June 1, 2005, along with another spotted leopard, Kayla. Police officers had confiscated the duo in Long Island, New York, while responding to a domestic disturbance call. Authorities transferred the pair to the Brookhaven Wildlife and Ecology Center in Holtsville, New York. Multiple moves can cause any animal great stress. The six-month-old cubs suffered from relocation anxiety, evident in their lack of appetite and skittish behavior.

The felines were neutered while living at Brookhaven, and preparations were made to transfer them to EFRC. Later that month, Jean Herrberg made the long drive to bring the cubs to their new home.

On their arrival at EFRC, the leopards moved into the director's house, and it was during their stay there that their personalities began to emerge. We dubbed one of the cubs George because his inquisitive nature reminded us of Curious George. His inquiring mind made him want to experience everything in his new environment. The other cub's radiant color reminded us of a goldenrod flower—hence the name Rodney.

EFRC introduced George and Rodney to Navi, a black leopard who was roughly the same age as the brothers. The two new cubs enjoyed Navi's company, and this made their transition to life at EFRC easier. The three made an adorable trio.

George and Rodney, April 5, 2009

George, February 8, 2008

Rodney, June 11, 2006

In April 2007, Rodney broke one of his canine teeth, and his jaw swelled up. Two EFRC staff transported him in EFRC's van to the University of Illinois Veterinary Teaching Hospital in Champaign, Illinois. On May 16, immediately after Rodney arrived, Dr. Sandra Manfra Marretta, DVM, a faculty member specializing in canine and feline dentistry, performed the first part of a two-part root canal procedure. Two weeks later, on May 30, she finished the procedure, and Rodney was given a round of antibiotics to ensure that infection did not set in. He completely recovered but at a cost of $1,922.70. This is just one example of the kind of veterinary expense a rescue center incurs in taking care of exotic felines.

Both cats love to entertain staff and visitors by performing acrobatic stunts, although Rodney is less frenetic than George. Jumping from platform to shelter or hanging from the enclosure fencing provides hours of fun for this duo. If you spend time observing George and Rodney, you will see how silly they can be. If you are present at feeding time, you will develop a clear understanding of just how powerful they can be. They may be relatively small, but their thunderous vocalizations have the potential to scare the living daylights out of you.

Rodney, September 21, 2008

George, September 10, 2006 (above)
Rodney and George, May 29, 2006 (below)

Jafar, a male tiger, arrived from Houston, Texas, on April 6, 2000, covered in blood and scared to death. Texas authorities had confined a sedated Jafar in a small wooden box and placed him in the back of a truck. Imagine waking up in a dark, loud, and terrifying environment and traveling more than fifteen hours in a box. Jafar did the only thing he knew to do. He tried to escape. He thrashed around in that box until it was almost more than he could bear. EFRC made complaints to the USDA about this inappropriate method of transportation.

In spite of his difficult journey, Jafar has developed a wonderful personality at the Center. "Friendly," "sweet," "humorous," and "playful" are just a few adjectives that describe Jafar. His best friend is his neighbor Hunter. They spend many hours chuffing to each other through the fence. Socializing as they do provides both with valuable stimulation.

Jafar also enjoys sledding in the winter. He accomplishes this feat in several steps. Step 1: flip water tank to expel water. Step 2: allow water to freeze. Step 3: stand on top of inverted water tank and go for a ride.

Despite Jafar's friendly personality, he exhibits intense food aggression. Placing Jafar's dinner in the middle of his enclosure allows him to eat in peace without visitors or his feline friends disturbing him.

You will encounter Jafar's enclosure near the end of the tour.

Jafar, August 19, 2007

Jafar, February 24, 2008 (above)

Jafar, June 20, 2008 (above), and December 30, 2007 (below)

JAGGER

Tiger

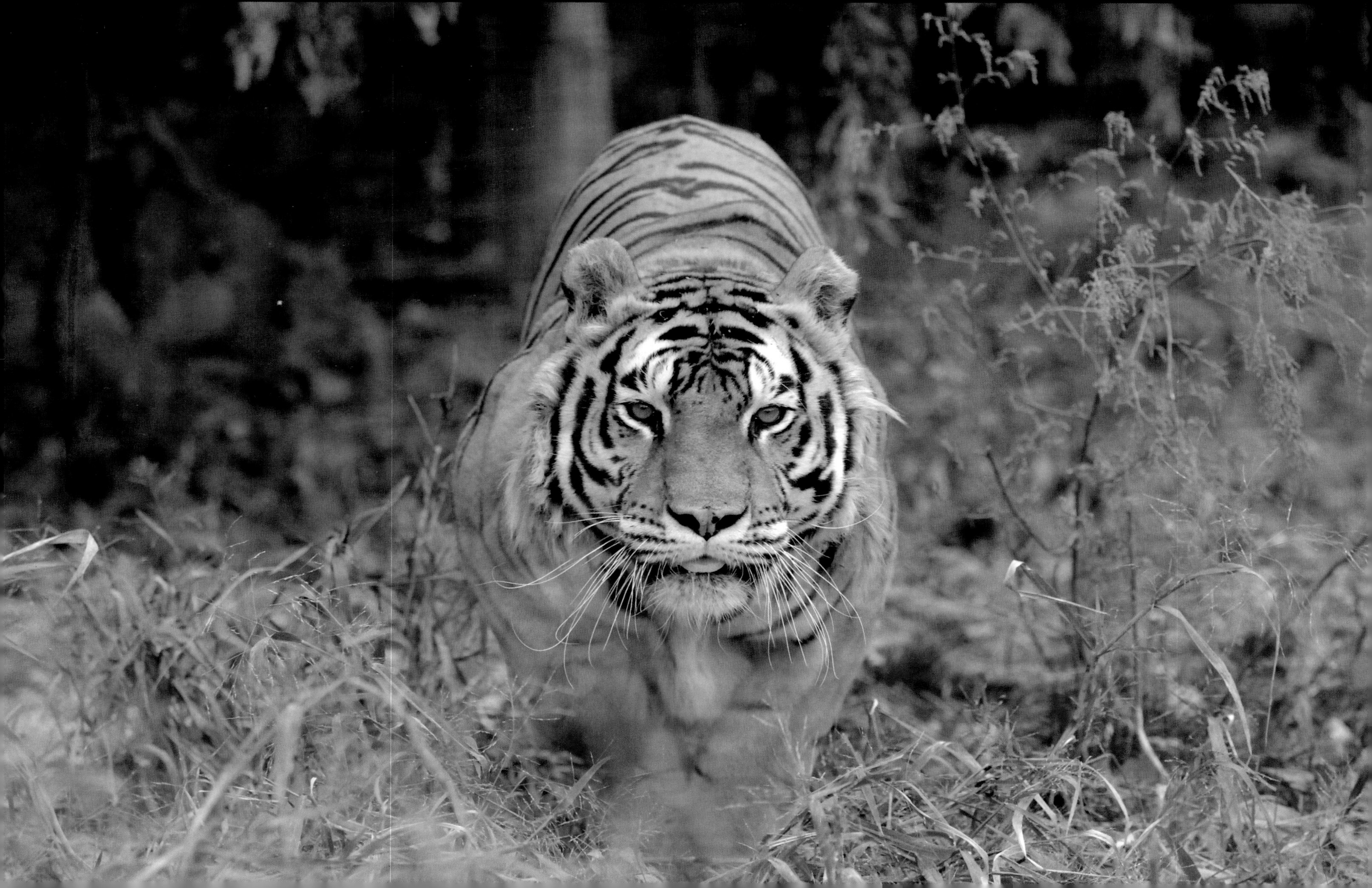

Jagger's life story attests to the tragedy that owning an exotic feline can lead to. While in Las Vegas, Jagger killed one of his trainers. We know he left Las Vegas with his owner after the accident, but the two years between then and when his owner abandoned him in Minnesota remain unaccounted for. He was taken into a facility in Minnesota, but, unfortunately, the facility owner would only feed Jagger. Because of his past behavior, she was afraid to clean his enclosure. When Jean Herrberg arrived in Minnesota, she found Jagger living in filth. He was underweight and had drainage from one ear, several broken teeth, a dull coat, exposed vertebrae and a very bad attitude, especially toward men. But who could blame him? He was a miserable tiger in a miserable situation.

He was transported to the veterinary hospital at the University of Illinois, where he received a complete evaluation. With proper treatment and medicine, the true Jagger began to emerge. Initially placed in temporary housing, he has since moved into a large, beautiful enclosure. Plentiful vegetation, large trees, a huge water tank and lots of shade allow the happy and contented Jagger to enjoy his days at EFRC.

Jagger also demands attention from staff. Even though he displays intense food aggression, he prefers to be hand-fed. Because of digestion problems, he cannot eat red meat. Therefore, staff push chicken through the fence. Needless to say, feeders try to stay very aware of Jagger's teeth.

Because of Jagger's history, he is not on the public tour.

Jagger, October 12, 2007

Jagger, February 10, 2006

Jagger, May 2, 2006

KING, JASMINE, AND LAUREN Lions

King, a male lion, and Jasmine, a female lion, arrived separately at EFRC in the fall of 2001. Along with Lauren, their daughter, they have become among the most popular animals at EFRC with visitors and staff. Their story is told in *Saving the Big Cats* (McCloud, 2006). They are included here by popular request.

Since *Saving the Big Cats*, Lauren's personality has continued to emerge. Even though she is being raised in captivity, Lauren's hunting instincts have developed as they would in the wild. These hunting instincts manifest themselves when toddlers and small children visit Lauren's enclosure. Staff and volunteer tour guides can recount numerous times when they caught Lauren watching these small guests with great interest. Since Lauren is content and well fed with horse meat or beef, the little visitors only provide visual stimulation.

King, Jasmine, and Lauren's enclosure is located at the bottom of the steps near where the tour begins.

King, February 9, 2002

King, June 10, 2007

Lakota, a male bobcat, arrived on July 8, 2006, with Kisa (a lion) from Ainsworth, Iowa. The private owner voluntarily surrendered the felines because she could not properly care for them. Born on April 30, 2002, Lakota was full-grown when he arrived, weighing in at twenty-five pounds.

After Lakota had acclimated to his new home, staff inadvertently began feeding him multiple times a day, as he would beg for food from anyone who walked by his enclosure—not necessarily because he was hungry but because he enjoyed the attention. Once staff saw what he was up to, he was put on a regular feeding schedule.

You will come to Lakota's enclosure halfway through the tour. Sometimes he is difficult to spot: in the spring and summer, Lakota's fur is brown, while in the fall and winter it is gray. He relies on his camouflage to stalk staff and visitors. Do not be surprised if, after you arrive at his enclosure, you become his intended prey.

Lakota's appearance, like that of all bobcats, can be deceptive. Although he looks cute and cuddly and resembles a house cat, he is solid muscle and could cause serious damage to a human or a house. And like the other big felines, he also sprays. Because of these traits, bobcats do not make suitable house pets.

Lakota, March 9, 2007

Lakota, March 9, 2007

Lakota, May 3, 2009

Near death, Lanky was rescued in June 2004 during a federal seizure in Ohio. When we arrived for the confiscation, we discovered the male Canada lynx in a wire cage placed on concrete. There was no water in his cage, nor did the cage receive any relief from the summer sun. Seeing Lanky's distress, keepers provided him with shade and water until they could load him into his transport cage and head for EFRC.

Lanky appeared to be elderly and showed definite signs of neurological impairment. Because of his precarious health, he underwent a complete medical evaluation when he arrived. Although Lanky's blood-work results were within normal limits, the examination revealed certain complications. He had two abscessed molars, which the veterinarian removed, and he only weighed eighteen pounds. If Lanky were to survive, we would have to monitor him very closely, ensuring proper fluid and food intake. The desire for him to survive competed with worry over what kind of future he would have. No one knew if the damage done was surmountable.

Lanky did not disappoint. He slowly gained weight, and once inside his new enclosure, he explored every inch.

Three years into his stay at EFRC, Lanky is doing well. Although he has developed vision problems with age, he continues to enjoy life. Enclosure accommodations allow Lanky to maneuver freely in

Lanky, May 17, 2008

Lanky, May 20, 2005

Lanky, July 31, 2004

his surroundings. Leaping up to his table to take a sniff of fresh country air—as well as his daytime stretching routine—keeps him well exercised.

Because of Lanky's background and health conditions, he is not on the public tour. His enclosure is located near the director's house. Special event attendees and overnight guests might see Lanky. If you do happen to catch sight of him, we warn you: once Lanky gains access to your heart, he takes up permanent residence. Hopefully, Lanky's precious face and unforgettable story will compel everyone to continue the fight for these beautiful exotic felines.

Lanky, May 17, 2008

LEROY AND LUKE

Leroy, March 9, 2007

Luke, March 4, 2005

Leroy and Luke, male pumas and longtime residents of EFRC, arrived in October 1995 and July 1998, respectively. Although both pumas came from the same place and arrived as adults, their routes to EFRC differed. We pieced together their histories and determined that Luke came to EFRC from a private owner in Illinois, while Leroy had at least two placements—a private owner and a Mississippi facility placement. It was after he'd arrived at the Mississippi facility that EFRC agreed to take him. Coming to his forever home at EFRC freed him from a future of uncertainty.

Luke's and Leroy's enclosures are located near the beginning of the tour. Seeing them in real life allows visitors to appreciate the true size of a male puma as well as the puma's true beauty and power. Pictures are not the same. During the spring and summer, visitors walk along Luke's and Leroy's enclosures hoping for a look. Because their enclosures are relatively large and abound with trees, tall grasses, and dense underbrush, during the summer it is next to impossible to spot the two. Even when cats are born into captivity, their instinct to stalk is ever present. Although Luke spends much of his time in his shelter, staff and volunteers can recount numerous occasions on which they searched for the boys only to find them lying just on the other side of the fence. When pumas move, you will not hear them unless they want you to hear them.

Leory and Luke are very skittish with the many humans in their lives. When feeding the boys, we have to be ready for grabby paws through the fence. This is not to say Luke and Leroy are unkind; they are just being pumas, and we love them for that.

When you arrive at their neighboring enclosures during your visit, you might spend a considerable amount of time looking for Luke and Leroy. Just remember, they could be right in front of you.

Lilly, a female puma, was found prowling around Hardy Lake State Recreation Area in southern Indiana. People reported her casually walking around and begging for food. When a Department of Natural Resources (DNR) agent approached her with a transportation crate, she walked in with only an enticement of a chicken leg quarter. Because of her ease with people, the DNR guessed she had been a pet. When no one came forward to claim her, Hardy Lake staff contacted EFRC which agreed to take her in. She arrived on November 30, 1997, at nine months of age.

EFRC wanted Lilly to have companionship, so the Center made two attempts to introduce her to fellow pumas, but she refused both offers. She preferred to be a single woman and avoid the hassle of others in her life.

Lilly is a sweet, outgoing, people-friendly puma who demands attention from staff. If you want to see her during your tour, you will more than likely have to look up. She spends most of her time on one of the elevated ledges in her enclosure. Unfortunately, during the summer, Lilly is very difficult to spot because of the dense vegetation in her enclosure, but you might hear her delightful purr.

June 2009 update: Tinker and Lilly were introduced and seem to be adjusting.

Lilly, December 7, 2007

Lilly, March 20, 2009

43

Madyson, May 28, 2007 (above)

Mirage, September 10, 2006 (above right),
and May 15, 2009 (below right)

MADYSON AND MIRAGE

Servals

Madyson and Mirage, a female and male serval, came to EFRC via Wisconsin and Las Vegas, Nevada, respectively. Madyson arrived on March 30, 2003, having been surrendered to EFRC by her owner, while Mirage, who had been found wandering the streets of Las Vegas on October 7, 2004, arrived on October 21, 2004.

Authorities surmised that Mirage was an escaped pet, but no one was surprised when the owner did not step forward to claim him. Because Mirage is an exotic feline, if someone did step forward, he or she could have been fined $1,000 and also could have been sent to jail for six months according to Nevada laws.

Mirage was taken in by the Dewey Animal Care Center in Las Vegas, but that center couldn't keep him and saw no option but euthanasia. News of his predicament spread and motivated concerned citizens to act. Mirage needed a new home immediately, and fortunately, Dr. Leslie Lisdell came to his rescue. She offered a sizable donation that would cover the costs of moving Mirage to EFRC. After EFRC submitted its credentials to the Clark County officials and was selected to house Mirage, an experienced volunteer flew to Las Vegas to bring Mirage to his new forever home.

Because servals do quite well when introduced to unfamiliar servals, we decided to introduce Mirage and Madyson. The introduction went smoothly, and so we were hopeful they would become fast friends. Subsequent observation of the two felines proved that our hopes were well-founded.

Mirage, May 15, 2009

The cohabitating servals quickly adjusted to their new home and lives at EFRC. Like house cats, exotic felines sometimes adopt the attitude of their enclosure mates. On arrival, Mirage possessed a sweet personality and longed for affection from staff. Moving in with Madyson changed all of that. Their tempers seem to have aligned. Both want very little to do with humans, and both voice their opinions freely. The way we see it, these servals have a reputation to uphold, so everyone accepts the duo's aloofness. And even though they present a cantankerous front, we believe they are kind-hearted cats deep down inside. They are loved in spite of their difficult attitudes, or maybe because of them.

Unfortunately, Madyson and Mirage are not on the public tour.

Mau's group currently includes seven tigers: Mau, Venus, Tigger III, Rajah, Taz, Dizzy, and Natas. Tigger III and Rajah are brothers, while Taz, Dizzy, and Natas—referred to as the Shy Girls—are sisters. Blending this group of seven tigers took time and patience, but it worked in the end, demonstrating animal tenacity and adaptability. Sadly, their story also illustrates that no matter how much staff, volunteers, supporters, and visitors love the cats, the damage done by abuse and neglect may never be reversed.

Mau is the offspring of Big Boy and Layla, while Venus came from a photo booth business when she was approximately five months old. Tiger cubs quickly grow too large and come to present too much of a danger to last very long at a photo booth operation. Unfortunately, photo booth owners want to dispose of the inconvenience and danger. Only a lucky few are rescued, and Venus was one of them.

The Shy Girls arrived on December 1, 2001, reeling from the harsh circumstances of their short lives. Ripped from their mother at three months of age, they were sold for $25 each at an Ohio animal auction. In the first month after their sale, they went through three different homes. Unfortunately, multiple placements of exotic animals is common and can cause them great stress. Even if an animal eventually finds a peaceful and stress-free home, the effects of his or her early life can linger forever.

EFRC knows nothing about the Shy Girls' first two placements but surmises that the second owner assumed the tigers would be easy to manage. The third owner took them hoping to use them in a traveling classroom program. Although tigers are cute and cuddly when they are born, they quickly become unmanageable furry balls of destruction. When the third owner contacted EFRC, we agreed to take them. Their fourth and final relocation would be to their forever home.

The girls left Ohio on December 1, 2001. They were locked into a small dog crate and loaded into the back of a pick-up truck. As the truck sped down the road, tarps banged and crashed against the cubs' cage, terrifying them. When the traumatized Shy Girls finally arrived at EFRC, they were put in a quiet room away from other cats and visitors. This allowed us the opportunity to give the girls multiple feedings and pay close attention to their unique wants and needs. We hand-fed chicken to the tigers, hoping this would improve the cubs' social skills. Sadly, it didn't. Although the tigers would take the chicken, they would withdraw with it hissing. Undaunted, we continued to work with the Shy Girls while their new habitat was being constructed.

In March, with their enclosure completed, the girls received complete physicals and were spayed. When the girls had adequately healed from their surgery, we moved them to a holding area next

Mau's group, February 15, 2005

to Mau and Venus. We hoped to see friendly signs between the five tigers, and we were not disappointed. Mau's duo quickly became a group of five, and the Shy Girls had two new feline friends.

The acclimation of the girls to humans has been slow in coming. When they were young, they would watch in amazement as their feline friends interacted with the keepers. They have permanent emotional scars from their early experiences and so tend to be difficult. Working with them tests the keepers' patience, but they deal with the sisters' behavior and love them in spite of it.

In April 2002, three more tigers made the life-saving trip to EFRC. Their road to the Center was as traumatic as that of the Shy Girls. Tigger III, Rajah, and Abby were born on September 10, 2001. Their owner illegally sold them across state lines to two or three different facilities. Abby arrived first at EFRC. Confiscated by Pennsylvania authorities, she arrived at one month of age weighing only seven pounds, eleven ounces. EFRC was her fourth home in four weeks! She was suffering from bloody diarrhea, had burned paws (possibly from bleach or urine), and was missing fur from her frail little body. During the six weeks she lived at EFRC, staff nursed her back to a healthy twenty pounds and fell in love with her.

EFRC wanted to provide Abby a full-time home, but authorities forced EFRC to send her to Baltimore, Maryland, because she was part of an ongoing federal investigation. By selling her and her brothers over state lines, the owner had violated the Endangered Species Act. The trio was held at a zoo while the legal proceedings played out. Although Abby was reunited with her brothers, EFRC staff worried about the stress yet another relocation could cause her. She had come so far while at EFRC, and staff feared she might regress.

Finally, in April 2002, the Baltimore authorities contacted EFRC to discuss relocation plans for the three siblings. To the staff's joy, everyone agreed the three tiger cubs should remain together. EFRC staff left Center Point on April 3 to bring the trio to their forever home. When they arrived at EFRC, the tigers were housed in a temporary enclosure near the director's house. This gave staff time to become reacquainted with Abby and familiar and comfortable with her brothers. The three also received medical evaluations. The veterinarian determined that Tigger was suffering from anemia and had a horrible case of fleas. After they had been treated and were healthy, the three tiger cubs were transferred to their new habitat and introduced to the Shy Girls, Venus, and Mau. The eight tigers became the best of friends. Sadly, Abby passed away on September 15, 2002. Even though we had her for only a short time, she stole our hearts and will never be forgotten.

To watch the tigers in their large enclosure is entertaining. The Shy Girls rarely approach the fence—when they do, it is with much

Mau's group, March 21, 2007

trepidation, and they are usually hissing or growling at the same time, but the other four crave attention from staff. They come to the fence expecting affection. Running, jumping, climbing, and tackling are just a few of their antics. Their area includes a climbing tower, water tanks, a towering tree, and a large hill. This hill gives the tigers a perfect spot from which to scan their environment.

If visitors attend a special event, they will have the opportunity to see Mau's group. When guests spot Tigger III, they assume he is either a tigon or liger because he does not have the typical striping pattern of a tiger, but he is a full-blooded tiger, as is his striped brother. Tigger, who has an easygoing personality, assists staff during feeding time. Because the Shy Girls loathe human beings, they do not always come when called. If the girls still refuse to come af-ter more calling, Tigger plods up to them and gives them a nudge. Slowly, the girls make their way down to the smaller enclosure. Once all seven are contained, staff go in to clean the enclosure and then leave the tigers their dinner.

EFRC hopes that visitors who observe Mau's group see seven beautiful tigers and that after they hear the tigers' heart-rending story, they share that story with others. Never again will these tigers be hungry, put in a speeding truck, or confined in a small area. To be able to run free, with the sun shining down on their orange coats and the wind blowing their tails, and to have enough food and water every day is what these tigers crave and deserve. Having made their way to EFRC, they will only know peace until their time on earth is completed.

Mau's group, March 21, 2007

MAX AND KISA

Tiger and Lion

Max, a male tiger, arrived on November 14, 2005, at five weeks of age, from a substandard Indiana facility. Max weighed seven pounds at the time and was a tiny ball of fur. As he grew, EFRC began to worry that something was wrong with his eyesight. Staff wondered if he might have cataracts, as those are common among tigers. EFRC transported Max to Chicago to see Dr. Paul Gerding, Jr., a veterinary ophthalmologist at Eye Care for Animals. The examination revealed minor cataract impairment, but Dr. Gerding determined surgery was not needed at that time. His condition is being monitored.

Because Max was so young when he arrived, he first lived at the director's house. He needed multiple feedings throughout the day and night, and that meant that multiple people entered his life. As a result of this early and sustained exposure to humans, Max has become one of the most people-friendly cats EFRC has ever encountered. Although Max had learned to love people, EFRC knew he needed a feline friend. When the Center received a call regarding a young female lion, Kisa, staff jumped at the chance to have her.

Eight-month-old Kisa arrived with Lakota, a male bobcat, on July 8, 2006. Staff placed Kisa in the small part of Max's enclosure and observed their initial encounter through the fence. Max chuffed immediately. Given this positive response, the decision

Max, February 15, 2008

Max, April 26, 2009

Max and Kisa, December 22, 2007

Max, July 19, 2009

Kisa, April 3, 2009

was made to move Kisa into Max's enclosure. Staff watched eagerly as the slide gate was opened. Initially, Kisa was hesitant to approach Max, but slowly an awe-inspiring friendship developed.

As Kisa grew, she began displaying walking difficulties. After observing her and consulting with staff, a veterinarian diagnosed Kisa with ataxia, a neurological dysfunction. Unfortunately, no cure exists for her condition, but she began a treatment regimen of vitamin A capsules. Moderate improvements were noticed in her gait. EFRC also modified her enclosure by adding intermediate levels to the climbing tower and shelter.

As Max and Kisa mature, their personalities are shining through. There are no strangers in Max's life, and everything in his world leads to a new adventure. After discovering a snake visitor in their enclosure, the felines ran around in circles and jumped back and forth trying to determine what this slithery creature might want from them. Both come to the fence for attention, although Max can be elusive at times—especially when he is at the top of his climbing tower. It just seems too much work to jump down. Max's gentle demeanor with Kisa is uplifting to see. He loves her with all his heart.

Hopefully, you will meet Max and Kisa during your tour.

Kisa, January 3, 2009

The Ohio office of the FWS confiscated Navi, a declawed black leopard, in February 2005 because she had been sold illegally across state lines. After taking possession of her, authorities contacted EFRC to see if the Center could accommodate her. EFRC said yes.

By the time Navi arrived, she was twelve weeks old. For the first three months of her stay, she boarded with the director. Some would say the result of that special attention is a spoiled leopard, while others would say it is a sweet and loving leopard. It is true that Navi demands attention from the few people she loves. If the keepers walk by Navi and mistakenly fail to acknowledge her presence, her vocalizations point out their oversight.

Navi enjoys time spent with her enclosure mates, George and Rodney. The trio have a harmonious relationship, although Navi retreats when the boys roughhouse. She routinely climbs to a platform to rest and watch arriving and departing visitors.

Be sure to acknowledge Navi when you visit EFRC. It might be best to tell her how pretty she is and how happy you are to see her.

Navi, March 22, 2009

Navi, April 12, 2009

Navi, March 25, 2007

SANTASIA AND SEMINOLE

Tigers

Seminole, January 4, 2009

Santasia, May 16, 2009

Tiger siblings Santasia and Seminole arrived at EFRC in early 2007. They were born on March 13, 1998, and sold four days later to an Ohio couple. Paperwork related to the sale consisted of a receipt for $250 and a handwritten note stating that the buyers had received demonstrations and written and verbal instructions regarding the care of two four-day-old tiger cubs.

In Ohio, Santasia and Seminole lived in a residential area without a perimeter fence and near a school. This setting had the potential for disaster. According to the local newspaper, the *Pataskala Standard*, fearful neighbors complained to the Pataskala city council. A next-door neighbor stated he could not go outside because the tigers were so close to his property.

After Santasia and Seminole's owner died, EFRC agreed to take the siblings and provide them a lifelong home. On the day of the

rescue, volunteers met two EFRC staff to assist with loading the felines into small circus cages and then into a truck for the ride home. When the duo arrived, they were placed in temporary housing off the tour route.

The siblings have proven to be friendly tigers who offer chuffs to anyone who walks by their enclosure. Though they are people-friendly tigers, sibling rivalry sometimes rears its ugly head. Santasia appears to be the dominant cat, but Seminole forcefully voices his opinion during feeding time. He likes his meat.

Santasia and Seminole now live in a new, larger enclosure that visitors pass on the public tour. As you move past their location, be sure to listen closely. You will probably hear the duo discussing your presence in their home.

Seminole and Santasia, December 31, 2008

SASSY, KING, JR, AND ULURU   Leopards

Sassy and King, spotted leopards, arrived at EFRC in June 2004 after a court-ordered seizure of twenty-nine exotic animals from an Ohio exotic animal farm. In addition to EFRC, animal sanctuaries in Colorado, North Carolina, and Pennsylvania were selected by the USDA to house the rescued animals with the stipulation that the animals not be bred or euthanized. Gathering at the farm, the sanctuary workers prepared to rescue fifteen tigers, eight lions, three leopards, one puma, one lynx (Lanky), and one Himalayan sun bear.

Deplorable conditions at the farm had been reported since 1983, when a Bengal tiger had mauled and killed the owner's two-year-old son. Although the owner was initially charged with child endangerment and involuntary manslaughter, charges against him were dropped in 1984. Despite the savage attack, the USDA granted the owner a license to keep and exhibit exotic animals at carnivals and county fairs.

There were two more tragedies at the exotic animal farm. In 1997, the owner's two-year-old grandson was attacked, and in 2006, a white tiger attacked a federal inspector. Both victims survived these attacks.

In 2002, the county health department cited the farm as a public health nuisance. The USDA also filed forty-seven charges related to the unclean and unsafe living conditions of more than sixty

JR, August 10, 2008

JR, August 10, 2008

Uluru, September 9, 2006

61

Uluru, April 3, 2009

JR, April 3, 2009

animals located on the farm. Because of these charges, the court permitted inspectors to bear arms during unannounced inspections. Finally, in 2003, county officials ordered all animals removed from the farm. After the owner's appeals to keep his animals were denied, the judge stated "enough is enough" and demanded that the board of health's order be enforced immediately. Although this order was carried out, the owner managed to stay in business, and county officials are still having trouble with him. The *Beacon Journal* reported on March 4, 2008, that the conditions of the cages and enclosures of eight bears, three tigers, and one lion on the farm were the subject of yet another investigation.

Removal of the animals began on an early morning in June 2004. Owing to the large number of animals that had to be loaded, the rescue took all day. Raw chicken was not enough to lure all the frightened animals into portable cages for loading—one lion had to be sedated. This rescue is an example of how difficult loading frightened animals can be. The process is arduous and takes patience and perseverance.

When Sassy was confiscated, she was one and a half months pregnant. Although EFRC spays and neuters their felines, when a cat arrives pregnant, we prepare for cubs. Because she was pregnant, EFRC separated her from King, the father. She was placed behind the director's house in two connected transport cages that included an enclosed shelter in which she could give birth. On July 25, 2004, Sassy gave birth to two spotted leopards, JR, a male, and Uluru, a female. Sassy performed her motherly duties with ease. Three weeks after their birth, JR and Uluru moved to the director's house. Because EFRC is not a breeding facility and does not have proper enclosures for nursing females and their cubs, cubs have to leave their mothers at an early age. Also, all cats require medical evaluations and yearly vaccinations and may have to undergo other procedures, and it is much easier to work with an animal that is accustomed to human contact. While living in the director's house, JR and Uluru were bottle-fed for three months. They were both playful cubs, but Uluru was the feistier of the two. After hours of roughhousing, the cubs would cuddle together while sleeping.

JR and Uluru are easily distinguished by size. JR weighs in at a hefty one hundred pounds, while a petite Uluru weighs approximately seventy pounds. The two share traits with their parents. Sassy and JR are similar in nature. Both become very excited during feeding time and require a great deal of attention from staff. Of course, because they are leopards, they lack knowledge of attention-getting rules, and extra fencing had to be added to their enclosure on account of their grabby claws. King and his daughter are quite the lazy leopards. They enjoy spending their day observing the world and sleeping.

The leopards are not on the public tour because when they arrived there were no enclosures available on the tour route. Sassy and King share an enclosure in the Hills section while JR and Uluru are currently located in the Field area.

On February 20, 1996, six-month-old Sheba arrived at EFRC accompanied by fellow puma Sampson. Sheba and Sampson were relocated three times. They first came to EFRC on November 11, 1995, after they were taken from their owner. A month later, they were returned to the owner. But the owner could not obtain a license to house them, and so they made their final move back to EFRC on February 20, 1996. Shortly after their arrival, EFRC received a call regarding another young puma, Skyler. Since the three pumas were close in age, staff hoped they could become enclosure mates. When Skyler arrived on March 2, 1996, introductions ensued with favorable results. The trio quickly became friends and moved to their new enclosure, which you come to near the end of the tour.

Tragically, in January 2005 Sampson and Skyler succumbed to listeriosis, a contagious disease. Mercifully, Sheba did not contract the illness, but there was worry that grief might send her into depression, and so staff showered her with attention and affection. Several visitations a day slowly helped to alleviate Sheba's sadness, and her genial personality reemerged.

When you arrive at Sheba's enclosure, listen closely. One of two things might stir the air: a puma chirp or a purr to end all purrs. If you are fortunate enough to hear the famous purr, you will just have to smile.

Sheba, October 22, 2005

Sheba, October 22, 2005

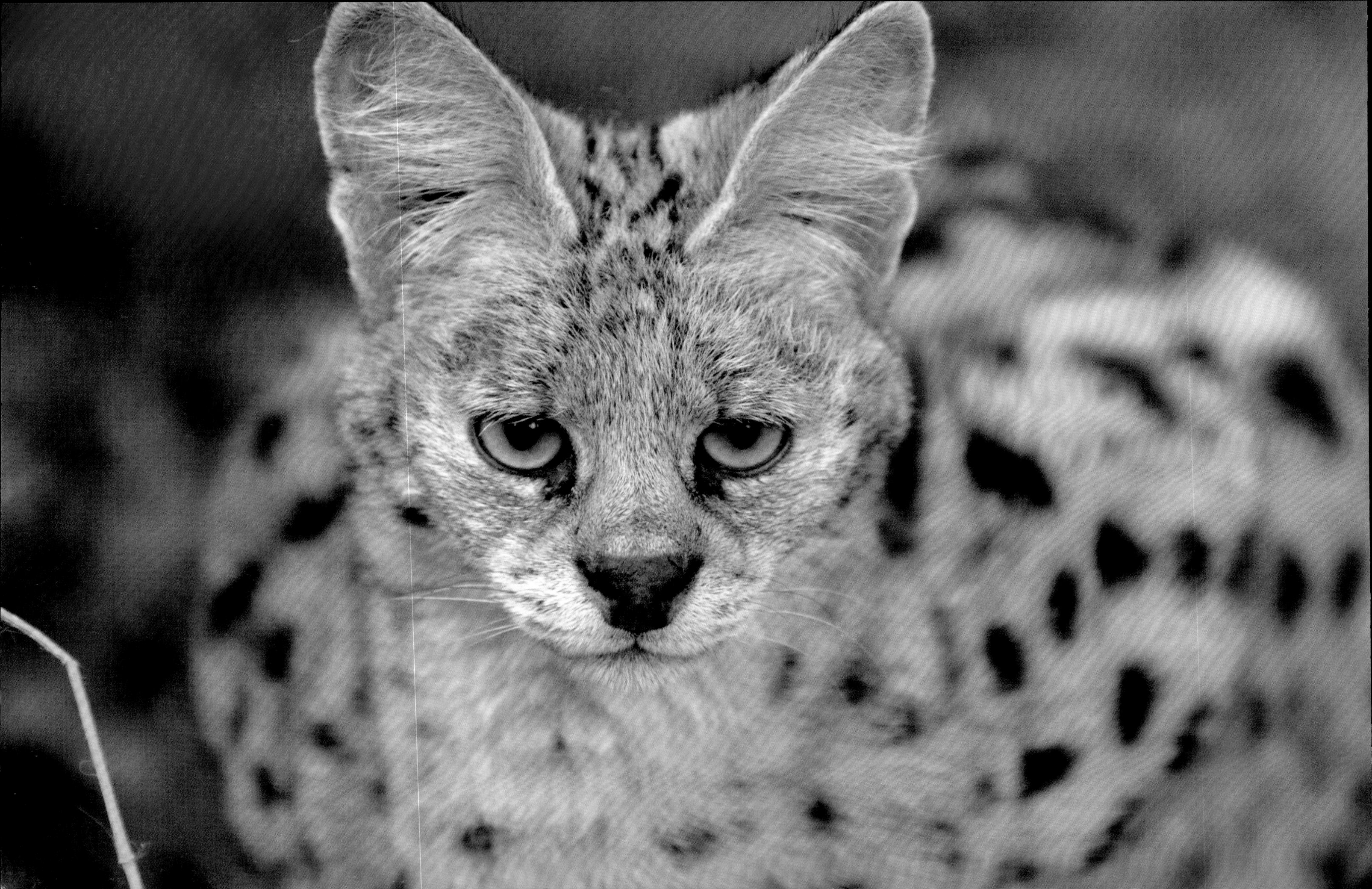

In December 2007, the New York State Department of Environmental Conservation requested accommodations for two confiscated cats, Shiloh, an African serval, and Alex, a bobcat.

Initially, Shiloh lived with the EFRC director because of poor health. Her coat appeared dull, and she refused to groom herself. During a medical examination, the veterinarian discovered that Shiloh had suffered a broken jaw at some point during her life. This was a possible explanation for why she wouldn't groom herself.

Shiloh's health improved and she experienced new adventures. Because she had lived with felines in the past, she was introduced to a male serval, Boi Pello. Introducing unfamiliar felines to each other can be difficult, but unlike lions and tigers, servals accept new enclosure mates quite easily. Shiloh has grown to love Boi Pello, but her feelings have not been fully reciprocated.

You will encounter Shiloh and Boi Pello as soon as you walk in the gate. Because Shiloh uses the enclosure foliage for privacy, you might need to spend some time searching for her. If you do find her, she will probably greet you with a hiss. That is just her way of saying "Welcome to my home."

Shiloh, April 5, 2009

Shiloh, September 21, 2008

The tale of Sumara and Sumira illustrates the catastrophes that can occur when people who are not qualified to take care of exotic felines choose to own them.

Their Beaver Dam, Kentucky, owner contacted EFRC requesting that the Center take the two male tigers. He could not control them. They had escaped from their primary enclosure two times in less than one week, although they did not manage to get outside the perimeter fence. The residential setting made the situation extremely dangerous and could have led to disaster for the nearby humans or the tigers or both.

Realizing the urgency, EFRC agreed to take the tigers. Despite snowstorms and ice storms, we were determined to leave immediately and mustered the rescue crew as quickly as possible. Unfortunately, plans do not always proceed as one would like. On the morning of the expected departure, we discovered a broken liftgate on the rental truck, which resulted in a twenty-four-hour delay. During these twenty-four hours, the tigers escaped for a third time.

After a four-hour drive on icy roads, EFRC staff arrived to find the tigers housed in an inadequate enclosure surrounded by an inadequate perimeter fence. The enclosure was wall-to-wall mud and did not contain straw or drinking water.

We successfully coaxed an agitated Sumira into the transport cage with an enticement of fresh straw and a deer leg. Unfortunately, Sumara was too afraid to follow. We had no choice but to immobilize him with a tranquilizer dart. When he was hit with the dart, Sumara charged the perimeter fence. The power of his charge broke the weak wooden supports, which created a very dangerous situation. The rescue workers could have found themselves in the position of having to kill the tiger in order to protect themselves. Fortunately, though, Sumara went down with the second dart. While he was sedated, we were able to examine him, immunize him, and load him into the truck for the trip home.

When Sumara and Sumira arrived at EFRC, they were placed in very temporary housing. Because funds were not available to build them a permanent enclosure, the director began the daunting process of relocating them to a private conservation center in Florida. Finally, in the spring of 2008, Sumara and Sumira arrived at the White Oak Conservation Center in Florida to find a twenty-one-thousand-square-foot enclosure with a waterfall, a pond, and tall trees for shade. Although EFRC wanted to keep these two beautiful tigers, staff know Sumara and Sumira are happy in their new home.

Raja Girl, July 4, 2006

Tahoe, December 17, 2006

EFRC felines come from all different kinds of owners, some better than others. Tahoe and Raja Girl's owner was, without a doubt, the most appalling. According to the LaPorte County, Indiana, prosecutor's office, the owner received a one-hundred-year prison sentence for two counts of child molestation in November 2002. While he was only charged with two counts, prosecutors estab-

lished that he molested more than 120 boys during a span of thirteen years. Along with Tahoe and Raja Girl, this owner had housed pumas and bears on his rural property.

After the owner headed to prison, a local veterinarian contacted EFRC to see if the Center could house Tahoe and Raja Girl. According to paperwork, Tahoe is Tony I's offspring. Although there are few details about Raja Girl's history, paperwork shows she was born in Colorado. When the tigers arrived on December 6, 2000, they appeared to be in good health. Unfortunately, Tahoe's health began to decline. He had arrived weighing 437 pounds, but by February 22, 2001, he had dropped to 379 pounds and had become quite lethargic. Staff could not determine the reason for the weight loss and changes in Tahoe's behavior, and so he was taken to the University of Illinois for a full medical evaluation. Blood tests suggested he was suffering from anemia. Moving exotic felines can cause the animals great stress, and with stress can come illness. Because of this, staff monitor new arrivals closely. Tahoe was treated for his anemia, which led to increased energy. He grew comfortable with his new surroundings and began to enjoy his new life at EFRC.

Although the two tigers are people friendly, both exhibit food aggression. Tahoe displays his ferociousness when eating, which sets off Raja Girl, who reveals her aggression by charging the fence. Tigers will do that occasionally. When food is not around, Raja Girl spends much of her time in her water tank. Many tour guides tell stories of encountering Raja Girl lounging her day away in the water. Tahoe, on the other hand, is famous for his hairballs. Imagine a hairball one hundred times the size of a domestic cat's—it leaves a lasting impression.

Tahoe, January 3, 2009

Those in the United States who trade in exotic animals often lie about the animals' histories. Conflicting reports regarding how three tiger cubs ended up in New York led them to their new home at EFRC. Tank, TJ, and JB began their lives at a northern Indiana facility. In February 2006, Tank was born to two Siberian tigers. On May 14, 2006, brothers TJ and JB were born to a different set of tigers. When TJ and JB were fourteen days old and Tank was three months old, the northern Indiana facility transported the trio to New York, where an unlicensed couple took possession of them. Were the tigers sold or donated to the New York couple? No one knows for sure. Because the couple did not possess a license and the tigers were possibly sold illegally over state lines, the New York authorities ended up confiscating the three tigers in August 2006. At this time, authorities took the tigers to the Seneca Park Zoo while the couple awaited the court's ruling regarding the cubs' fate. The court ordered that the tiger cubs be permanently removed from the unlicensed couple's home, so plans were made for their last relocation. They were coming back home to Indiana.

Because EFRC had a working relationship with the New York authorities, the Center happily agreed to take Tank, TJ, and JB. After New York agreed to pay the transportation costs, two staff members made the long drive to retrieve the trio and bring them back.

JB, November 10, 2006

TJ and JB, November 10, 2006 (above and below)

TJ, November 10, 2006

TJ, August 25, 2007

When the three arrived on November 8, 2006, they were placed near the director's house in a recently vacated enclosure. Staff could not help but fall deeply in love with the six- and nine-month-old fluffy boys. Within days, their distinct personalities emerged. TJ and JB demonstrate their master stalking skills to visitors and staff. Tank, on the other hand, tends to hang toward the back of the enclosure, but he moseys to the fence when called. Their most noticeable trait, however, is their constant chuffing when greeting familiar and unfamiliar people. They love everyone, and everyone loves them.

Since the boys' enclosure is not located on the public tour, they can be seen only by overnight guests and during special events. When visitors encounter them for the first time, they tend to comment on the boys' girth. They seem to be as wide as they are long. Many assume that the trio, especially the brothers, eat more than their share, but they do not—they are on the same feeding schedule as the other felines. Their size is still a mystery, but one guess is that excess water is giving them their waddly appearance, as they prefer to take their food in the water tank.

The boys also provide hours of fun for overnight guests. Resting at the picnic table, the visitors watch the boys running around and roughhousing with each other. They also have the opportunity to hear the trio's affectionate chuffs.

This will not be the last enclosure for the boys. Because they have grown so big, they will move to a larger enclosure when funding permits.

The same week EFRC agreed to take Tank, TJ, and JB, the Center received two other calls regarding six more tigers. Lack of funds and space as well as transportation issues prevented EFRC from rescuing those tigers. Their fate is unknown.

JB and Tank, July 19, 2008

Tasha is a twelve-year-old puma with an unsettling past. In 1999, authorities seized her from a negligent owner near Bloomington, Indiana. Despite the mistreatment she had suffered, she arrived at EFRC at the relatively healthy weight of 110 pounds. Even though EFRC was prepared to offer Tasha a lifelong home, the DNR placed her back with the owner. When confiscated a second time in January 2001, her situation had become life-threatening, and she weighed only 66 pounds. She was emaciated and suffering from severe dehydration, and she was barely able to stand. Once at EFRC, she lived in the director's back bedroom, where she received nutrition throughout the day. After she had regained some of her strength, staff transferred Tasha to temporary housing outdoors near the butcher stand, where she continued to receive multiple feedings a day. Luckily, Tasha has reached her target weight and regained the strength a puma needs to be powerful.

EFRC wants Tasha to experience the peace and quiet she so deserves. Although she has grown accustomed to EFRC staff, she is afraid of unfamiliar people. Because of this, she is rarely seen by visitors on the tour.

Tasha, October 25, 2006

Tasha, March 21, 2008

Tinker, a twelve-year-old male puma, arrived at EFRC in September 2006 from northern Indiana. When the DNR learned of Tinker, they drove to his location every few days to evaluate him and his needs. Since the owners failed to obtain the appropriate permit, authorities ultimately confiscated Tinker. At this time, EFRC agreed to take him.

Two staff members drove to northern Indiana to transport Tinker to his forever home. When he first arrived at EFRC, Tinker was placed near the clinic so he could be observed, and then he was transferred to his new enclosure. It did not take him long to adjust to his surroundings or to reveal his sweet personality. Tinker enjoys interacting with familiar staff and always has a purr to offer.

Tinker also entertains guests with his favorite play toy, a deer head. Visitors watch—partly in disgust and partly in shock—as Tinker goes to town with his deer head. He picks it up by the ear, tosses it into the air, flings it to the back of his enclosure, pushes it around like a ball, and cuddles it like a baby.

Tinker's enclosure neighbors that of Lilly, a fellow puma. If visitors are lucky, they will arrive during feeding time for Tinker's presentation of "How to Play with a Deer Head."

June 2009 update: Tinker and Lilly have been introduced and seem to be adjusting.

Tinker, October 10, 2006

Tinker, December 14, 2008

The CNN headline read "Drug Zoo in Indiana." This is where we found Tony I and Patti (Patti passed away in 2006). The USDA contacted EFRC requesting that the Center take two tigers from an appalling facility that housed tigers, leopards, wolves, bears, drugs, and stolen guns. Arriving at the facility, we found sick and suffering big cats in tiny, filthy cages. Within these cages, we spied dirty water—or worse yet, no water—mud, dead rats, dead pigeons, and no food. As we surveyed the grounds, we found weak fencing and no perimeter fence. Because not all of the animals could be rescued, we left two hundred pounds of chicken on the driveway, hoping the owner would feed the remaining animals. Later, USDA officials reported the chicken lay in the driveway, rotting in the summer heat for the entire day.

When Tony arrived in 2002, he was twelve years old. One would never know he'd suffered twelve years of neglect, because his personality exudes joy and contentment. To this writer, he is the sweetest cat at EFRC.

Because of his age, Tony sleeps away his days in his large enclosure that visitors come to halfway through the tour. If visitors are lucky, he will greet them at the fence with friendly chuffs.

Tony I, September 24, 2006

Tony I, May 9, 2006

Tony I, May 5, 2007

Tony I, November 3, 2007

TONY III, OTI, KIERA, MAJAE, AND CODY

On August 25, 2008, EFRC staff drove one hour to a Greene County, Indiana, USDA-licensed breeding facility to rescue a black leopard. Seeing the atrocious conditions of the "not so bad" facility, staff realized that all the big cats there needed rescuing. But since staff were only prepared to bring home Majae, the four remaining cats had to be left behind.

After preparing transport cages, renting a truck, and convening a rescue crew, staff left on August 27, 2008, to rescue the four remaining emaciated felines. Majae, two tigers (Oti and Tony III), one lioness (Kiera), and one puma (Cody) had been living in what would turn out to be the worst conditions EFRC had ever encountered. Decomposing carcasses, bones, and feces littered the facility. The felines were housed in small, filthy, and structurally unsound cages with no water and no food. The facility did not have a perimeter fence. The cats had been without food and water for an unknown length of time, and every bone was visible to the naked eye. All of the cats had sores, external cuts, and patches of missing fur on their emaciated bodies.

During a rescue, the most difficult part can be loading the animals into the small transport cages. In this case, the tigers loaded with only an enticement of a bucket of clean water. Cody, the puma, was eager to leave the facility, so he also loaded quickly. Kiera, the female lion, however, proved to be difficult. Because she was hostile and aggressive toward the rescuers, she needed to be sedated. She went down quickly with the first dart. Staff then had

Kiera, May 23, 2009 (above), and August 15, 2009 (below)

Kiera, May 10, 2009

Majae, March 6, 2009 (above), and May 10, 2009 (below)

to crawl through a small hole cut into the side of the cage in order to remove her. During such rescues, staff struggle to come to terms with how a human being could deny the necessities of survival to these living, breathing animals.

The first stop after the rescue team and the cats left Greene County was the veterinarian's office. The vet was able to draw blood and perform a superficial examination on the still-sedated Kiera. In examining Cody, the puma, the vet discovered he had multiple dental infections.

After their arrival at EFRC, staff placed the five cats in temporary housing that permitted close monitoring of their progress and facilitated the process of feeding them multiple times a day. As the cats gained weight and their health improved, staff began moving them to their new enclosures. Majae, the black leopard, moved first. Kiera was next. Although, according to the owner, Kiera is fourteen, she behaves like a kitten. As visitors approach her enclosure, her curiosity gets the best of her. She peeks around a small tree trunk to look at the humans observing her new home.

Cody was administered a two-week round of antibiotics in an attempt to stabilize his condition enough for surgery. At the end of the two weeks, he underwent his first surgery to remove damaged canine teeth. Unfortunately, when the vet removed the first rotten canine tooth, his jawbone fractured because of the severe infection. Another round of antibiotics was ordered. A successful second operation was performed six weeks later.

The owner had intended to use Tony III and Oti as a breeding pair once they reached maturity. When EFRC rescued Oti, she was spared from a future of delivering multiple litters. Her time at EFRC will be spent eating, relaxing, swimming, and playing.

During a rescue such as this, emotions run high for the rescuers. Great joy in saving these cats mingles with great sadness in confronting the question of why they need to be saved. What kind of person treats animals in such a way? Rescuers also feel sorrow for the felines living in similar circumstances that are not reached in time. Bad choices lead to situations in which cats are left to suffer horrible lives, and there are too many to save and not enough resources to do the saving.

In late 2008, EFRC staff transported Cody to a puma facility in Minnesota.

Oti, April 3, 2009 (above)

Tony III, March 22, 2009 (below left), and March 29, 2009 (below right)

WILD BOYZ

When the shooting ceased on March 25, 1998, eight tigers were dead. The largest documented slaughter of endangered tigers was complete. A federal undercover criminal investigation known as Operation Snowplow, however, spared five tigers—known as the Wild Boyz—from this fate. Operation Snowplow would uncover a ring of breeders, dealers, haulers, taxidermists, and sport hunters seeking to profit from the murder of exotic felines, as well as from that of other exotic animals

This story began in the mid-1990s, when an exotic animal park opened in Crete, Illinois. Although the owner of the park stated on the USDA application that he was opening a roadside zoo, a chance meeting in early 1997 between him and the owner of an African hunting business resulted in the animal park becoming a killing field for exotic animals. Some animals who came to the park lasted less than a day.

After federal investigators received a tip in August 1997 regarding the possible killing of two tigers, two USDA investigators went to the exotic animal farm, where they found a trailer containing a fresh pool of blood. The investigators later discovered that the killers had shot the tigers in the trailer at point-blank range. After posing for pictures with their kill, the shooters paid the dealer $4,500 for the skins and thousands more for the taxidermist services. Investigators also found other animals living amid trash, old bones, and soiled bedding.

The killers discovered that money could be made not only from the pelts but also from the animals' meat. Tiger killing subsequently began in earnest. The FWS started working with an informant who provided information regarding possible killings at the animal farm. A small group from the FWS then went undercover, posing as potential buyers of the feline pelts. The undercover agents discovered that wealthy hunters purchased the tiger pelts for their trophy collections and that the meat went to a Chicago-area meat market.

At the conclusion of Operation Snowplow, numerous individuals from Illinois, Michigan, Missouri, Oklahoma, Arkansas, and Florida had been found guilty of a number of federal wildlife protection crimes. Punishments ranged from fines of up to $125,000 to five years in federal prison. The National Fish and Wildlife Foundation's Save the Tiger Fund and the Lacey Act Reward Fund split the $125,000.

This is just one example of the kind of despicable acts associated with the multibillion-dollar, worldwide exotic animal trade where animals are sold, bought, and traded and sometimes slaughtered for their pelts and flesh.

Nine years after the operation had begun and seventeen prosecutions later, the FWS asked EFRC to provide a stable and secure home for six tigers, three leopards, and one puma. The rescue was carried out in three stages. The initial visit to obtain a black leopard, Chester, gave us a glimpse of the difficulties we would face in rescuing the other nine. Although the second visit to rescue Ellie, a tiger, Bubbles and Ebony, leopards, and Aries, a puma, went smoothly, removing the final five tigers, the Wild Boyz, would prove to be the most challenging rescue EFRC had attempted to date. The Wild Boyz were located in a one-acre wooded enclosure. Because the tigers had been housed in this unattended en-

closure for at least seven years, the staff would have to maneuver around skulls and bones of deceased tigers, excrement, mud, and water. The pen did not have a perimeter fence or a shift cage that would have permitted moving the cats one at a time. Along with these difficulties, four of the five tigers were unapproachable and unmanageable. Although these were daunting obstacles, the tigers' fear aggression would prove to be the biggest hurdle of all.

At the end of March 2006, fifteen staff and volunteers gathered, along with law enforcement personnel and FWS officials, to begin the rescue. Success depended on the Wild Boyz being darted and downed simultaneously, at which point they would undergo complete medical examinations and be loaded onto the truck. By 7:20 AM, the first cat had been darted. Despite the tranquilizers, however, the tigers kept charging the fence. The tension mounted as the rescuers watched and waited. Sheriffs with rifles stood by ready to fire if necessary. Finally, four hours later, all five tigers had been immobilized, vaccinated, treated for parasites, and loaded into the truck for the long ride to their EFRC home.

Before their rescue, the Wild Boyz had never known any feelings other than terror. Now they will never again hear gunshots or be witness to other tigers dying. Never again will they live in filth. Never again will they be unloved, because they are cared for by a staff dedicated to their well-being. Their new enclosure is twice as big as any of the other EFRC habitats. Within their home they have a large pond, woods, grasslands, and a climbing tower. The only sounds they hear now are crickets, birds, and the roar of their fellow felines.

The Wild Boyz continue to astonish staff with their resilience. Because Ryker had had previous contact with humans, he does not run from the keepers. Charger has grown comfortable enough to walk into the small area of his enclosure when staff members are near. And although Trooper, Caesar, and TJ remain afraid of humans, they recognize that EFRC staff will not harm them and have started accepting the people in their lives from a distance.

Their pond gives them great enjoyment as do the Boomer Balls in their enclosure. Although staff have not witnessed the boys playing with the Boomer Balls, the balls have been found in several different locations in their enclosure. Despite the Wild Boyz's years of hell, with time, patience, and unending love, they have reached the point of contentment.

Owing to the Wild Boyz's background, they are not on the public tour, and only EFRC staff visit their enclosure. EFRC's goal is for these five cats to live out the remainder of their lives in complete peace.

Wild Boyz pond, February 5, 2006

Audra Masternak's Blog

Audra Masternak, a small-town girl who had lived her entire life in Albion, Michigan, graduated from Albion College in 2008. She spent the summer of 2008 at the Philadelphia Zoo and in the fall of 2008 began an internship at EFRC. As a way to keep her family updated after arriving in Bloomington, Indiana, she started a blog about her experiences at EFRC, which follows here.

Thursday, November 13

. . . and it begins . . .

Well, we left on time . . . perfectly packed by Don. Eight hours later, dinner, cars unpacked, room set up . . . and I'm alone . . .

First days are boring. Settling in and finding a spot for all my warm clothes is redundant. Grocery shopping the same in every town, city, and state around. I mapped out my stomping ground and set up my internet/cable tv (hey! no cable at home and slow net . . . sure, it's one of the first things I did!!!). A slow and relaxing day in a schedule that would become very demanding, cold, and lllllooonnnnng.

I don't work Mondays, but do every other day give and take. But Tuesday was great. My first day was cold and rainy but ultimately all of what I had expected: dirty, wet, cold, and SPECTACULAR! It consisted of hauling a lot of meat to near the two hundred "big" cats at the rescue center: tigers, lions, cougars, servals, ocelots, bobcats, Canada lynx, etc. Let me tell you, cleaning enclosures is a sinus clearer.

There is a baby at the center, a baby serval. He is very cute and very fluffy . . . looks more like a baby cheetah than a serval. I can't wait until we can play with him. For now he is bottle-fed and kept away from keepers and staff so he doesn't get any infections before he is vaccinated.

Friday, November 21

. . . communicate through roars . . .

So, around here there is always something to talk about. Lions are always roaring . . . one roars and the rest roar all around the rescue center. It is pretty cool . . . I really like being part of all the fuss . . .

This week was busy. Tuesday was a long day (probably pushing ten hours!) and was full of feeding, cleaning, putting up Christmas decor around the main path, and butchering. Every other day has been just as long . . . 8:30 AM–6ish PM.

About this butchering . . . I wasn't so keen on this in the beginning . . . swearing up and down (to myself, of course) that I would not help with the process. Number one reason, when the chest cavity is cut open it smells just rotten (seriously, your head is right there, and I would rather not be shot in the face with steamy, moist air). When I say rotten, I mean like stagnant, old sweet corn, mixed with chewed cud, digested intestinal air that really puts a gumball-size knot in your throat. However, I've gotten used to this smell (without having to use Vicks to mask the smell). Second, I guess it just took some time for me to realize that we were not killing these animals. They die from natural causes (pneumonia, cancer, age, weather) and if they were not used as meat for the cats they would probably just be buried and decompose in some field pit with other cows. It helps that you never see them alive. But today . . . today we got thirteen animals in to butcher! Although it sounds morbid, it is really great we have so much food for the cats! The weather has been warm, then cold, then rain, then cold, which makes farmers' cows and horses just keel over. Butchering is actually quite interesting. I've gotten to see a lot of anatomy. Really BIG anatomy. The size of a draft horse liver . . . HUGE! Lungs of a bull . . . HUGE! You just have to get used to it—take a deep breath and hope for an exhale, not an upchuck.

Besides that, I stepped in some cow poop (which really stunk), gave all 191 cats meds, wiped out on a cow leg in the cooler, and picked up a whole load of guts off the floor and held them in the Bobcat so we could dump them in the compost. . . . Never really held up guts before, but it was definitely something new and experience worthy. Gotta say this is no job for the weak-at-heart, squirmy-stomached, or slack.

Our favorite cougar, Cody, left on Tuesday . . . he was rescued with a group of five other cats and was claimed by a sanctuary in Minnesota. It was sad to see him leave. He had been living in the building since Labor Day. Every time you went near him he purred so loudly it sounded like a truck. He also LOVED to be [petted] and rubbed! It is awesome being able to pet a big cat . . . something I've dreamed of my whole life! Simply amazing.

A leopard, Angle (angel), also passed away this week. She passed on her own, without euthanasia. She was very skinny and had had a very hard life previous to the rescue center. At least she was comfy in a warm straw bed, with a huge chunk of meat in front of her.

Saturday, November 22

. . . the grim reaper at the foot of my bed . . .

Well, he wasn't here to take me away. And in fact, I didn't even see him, just smelled him. You may ask what exactly I am talking about . . . well, what I mean is . . . it is laundry day!!!

See my clothes reek. As I have previously stated, I work with big cats. I clean up their poop, feed them raw meat, and also help butcher meat and haul it . . . along with getting the occasional tiger spray and holding guts. This job is messy and, as you can guess, I am extremely fragrant when I arrive home.

Laundry is a job. Cleaning your clothes everyday is pointless, especially when they are going to get just as dirty and smell the same every day. Nine layers of clothes—Under Armour, then tight long-sleeve, tank top, T-shirt, long-sleeve loose T-shirt, tighter nonhooded sweatshirt, fleece, hooded sweatshirt, and vest—are a lot to wash day after day. Yes . . . the smell seeps to the very bottom layer too!

So what I do is take the nasty, dirty layer off at work and leave it in the single-wide trailer (where everyone else does too) to let them dry, and wear my other eight layers home, separate them, and let them air out a little. I wear the under layers for about a week and the top layers for three to four days depending on how stiff the caked-on mud/blood/gut juice/dry water is on my pants . . . you have to have some mobility!

I didn't used to leave my clothes at work. I actually used to put them on the chair in my room. They smell awful, and when I said the grim reaper was at the foot of my bed, I actually meant that my clothes smelled dead. I now only put my layers in my room, right next to my air freshener. Problem solved.

Anyway, today I did laundry since I got the day off. You wouldn't believe it, but my clothes actually come out almost spotless! Seriously, Tide does wonders!

Monday, December 1

. . . oh, the lions! . . .

So I have come to the conclusion that the lions are definitely, DEFINITELY not my favorite breed of cats. Sure, they are pretty and noble looking, but many are just rotten! I have not met one yet that I can say I like.

Sure, I feel terrible looking at their scars from previous owners or their short legs, stubbed down by deformities from malnutrition, but sometimes I just wish that they would take a little more into consideration what the workers feel . . . ha, never going to happen.

I would say there are, hmmm, give or take, forty-ish lions at the rescue center. And I ask no questions [about] why they are there, because you can surely tell why one would never want to keep them as a pet! WHY?!

Clancy is very annoying, always trying to stalk you and being more than difficult to shift to the other side of his enclosure (especially for females . . . he really dislikes girls!). Rake is so food aggressive he never thinks twice about whapping one of his five harem lionesses. King is nice, until he decides he doesn't want to be. Tao is just obnoxious. Of course these are the males, but frankly . . . the females are no better!

Rappie sounds like some sort of machine, a loud semi truck, Harley-revving lion. That is just her normal breathing. When you look at her she rumbles, her breath taking on a misty, fog state, and blows into your face. The Southern Belles, a group of seven lionesses, are so slow and spoiled. They always stick their paws out of the smallest cracks and try to paddle your leg with their paws . . . a paddle, by the way, is like getting hit with force by a boat paddle, not just an easy stroke through the water.

I'd have to say Kisa would be the closest to one that I like. She lives with Max, a male tiger . . . one of the largest at the center (about six hundred pounds). She loves to have rubs through the fence, but will get very upset when Max comes to get some attention too. She roars her stinky breath in his face. It is so funny to see six-hundred-pound Max shrug back and jump away from the neurologically impaired Kisa! (She has ataxia.)

I am sure a lot of their temperament is because they are lions and tend to be more aggressive and territorial in the wild. Many of these traits also show when they are in captivity. It really is amazing, the noises these beautiful cats make. When they roar, when they growl, even when they grumble, it rattles your chest. It seriously vibrates all your insides. I would say it is something everyone should experience once . . . hearing all the commotion, that is! I do like the lions: the roars, their manes, the prides they form. I suppose I should just be more specific in saying I just do not enjoy their attitudes.

Thursday, December 4

. . . the nine . . .

Since my blog is about my big cat experiences, I will follow the outline of my previous posts and stick with . . . big cats!

"The Nine," as we call them, are a group of nine tigers all in one huge enclosure, fully furnished with two and a half boxes, an electrical spool, and a pond! They are from several different rescues, but because of their young and close ages when they arrived, they ended up together.

This is one of my favorite groups to feed just because they create so much commotion before being fed! They moan and they groan and they chuff . . . sounding more like a herd of cows than a group of tigers! They climb around on their boxes and even play a game of leapfrog, jumping over each other to see who can get out first to get the "big thing."

The big thing is the large part of the meal. Large groups like the Nine will get a big thing and several small chunks strewn about their enclosure, which ensures that every cat at least gets one chunk. However, a chunk is probably three times the size of a normal dinner pot roast for us!

The Nine are all very different. You might think all tigers look the same or wonder even how we tell them apart. Well, their stripes are like finger prints . . . just as no two humans have the same fingerprint, so no tiger has the same stripe pattern. Many of the tigers are big (really big) and many are smaller. Some are timid and some are aggressive, some are very lovable and others would just like to "eat you for dinner."

Anyways, the Nine include: Beaker, Rose, Taj, Dinkum, Jesse, Emily, P da and two others . . . it is really hard to remember their names and which cage they belong to!

So today I took a movie of the Nine exiting the shoot to get food! . . . This is what I call a good game of leapfrog!

Tuesday, December 9

. . . Oti and Tony, homeward bound . . .

Oti and Tony are two tigers waiting eagerly for a new enclosure! The rescue center received a phone call Labor Day regarding a black leopard (Majae) who needed a new home. On arrival, Joe (owner of the center) decided we would not only rescue Majae, but a lion (Kiera), a cougar (Cody), and two tigers (Oti and Tony).

The condition these animals were in was the worst the rescuers had seen in years, if not ever. The cages were small, and the floor was covered in rotted and decaying carcasses, so decayed it was hard to tell what they were given to eat in the first place. Their water bowls were dry with dust on the bottom, evidence they had not received water in days.

Although the cats were badly starved and severely dehydrated, the owner seemed to not be alarmed as she parked her BMW in the driveway, neglecting to fill the several dry dishes outside.

Rescues like these are very heartfelt; it really makes you proud of helping these cats. They have all since been fattened up with proper diets and several have been medicated and even gone through surgery. Cody went to a sanctuary in Minnesota, but Kiera, Majae, Oti, and Tony still reside at the center. However, Oti and Tony are still awaiting their new enclosure!

Can you believe it takes anywhere from $15,000–$20,000 for initial cage costs!? Not including the time it takes to build one and all the donated supplies from friends of the rescue center! On Wednesday, their wish came true, and although we had to play musical cats, they finally received their new home!

It was a long day of trying to shift four cats into new enclosures. Seminole and Santasia had to come out of a temp cage and go into a brand new one . . . Seminole shifted easily, jumping immediately into the circus cage, and was driven a quarter mile to his new home. Santasia was a different story. It took her three hours to get into the circus cage! When we finally did move her she was so distressed, but very, VERY happy to be back with Seminole and to meet new neighbors (a couple of lions and a group of eight frisky tigers!).

It took six of us to roll Oti and Tony (already living in a temporary circus cage) to their new site; we opened the door . . . THEY SHOT OUT! They jumped right out and ran around their small, but better than a cage, new temp home. They played with their boomer ball, jumped on their tower, and ran after each other. It was AWESOME to see them running and playing . . . well worth the wait!

Sunday, December 14

. . . peek-a-boo with Tony . . .

I went to visit those crazy young cats we just moved, Oti and Tony. They are right near the front gate so just a jaunt away from where we put on new gloves.

They both greeted me with loud chuffs and nuzzling against the fence, acting as though they hadn't had human contact in years! Chuffs, by the way, are a greeting tigers do when they are saying "Hey! What's up!" It is a friendly greeting, very hard to explain . . . kind of sounds like "fuh-fuh-fuh-fuh" really fast, no voice, just air sound. Anyways, these guys are so nice, and they used to be the focal point of visitors walking in the gate, but their new enclosure does not allow them to see as many people as they used to.

So I greeted them back and scratched their faces through the fence. Oti walked away and into their box. Tony, however, proceeded to walk behind his climbing tower and peeked over. He bent his ears down, along with his head, and peered over the tower. I could only see the top of his fluffy noggin and just a smidgen of his amber-colored eyes.

I knew what this meant. A lot of cats at the center LOVE to play peek-a-boo, so I thought to myself maybe Tony does too and we just never knew because there is obviously nowhere to hide in a circus cage, especially when you are a four-hundred pound cat! What we do, for all the cats who will play, is go up to the fence (just like with little kids) and say "Where is Tony?! Where could he be . . . TONY!!" Then normally the cat will jump from where they are hiding and barrel into the fence, chuffing the whole way to you. It really is quite cute!!

So I did just that. I took a step from the door and turned around pretending to be looking for him . . . his eyes were following me.

I saw his head raise up. I turned around . . . he ducked down, just peering. I looked the other way . . . he raised his head up again. I pretended to leave. Tony jumps over the climbing tower and rams into the fence. Greeting me with nothing less than a LOUD chuff!

It was so cute. You almost expected him to be wagging his tail, tongue hanging out, and smiling with delight, as if he were a dog.

Chuff. Chuff. Chuff.

Sunday, December 28

. . . a big cat holiday . . .

. . . rhyme to 'twas the night before Christmas . . .

'Twas the holiday season and all through the rescue,
The cats were all roaring and chuffing a few.
Their bellies were full with large meaty meals,
and they hoped that all days would give such full feels.

The leopards were snug curled up in their straw,
The tigers all resting, not raising a paw.
The cougars in boxes, the bobcats in cedar,
The Christmas decor, it couldn't have been neater.

When out in the center there rose such a clatter,
All the lions started fussing, expressing the matter.
Away to the fence line, the tigers they dashed,
Servals went running as if lightning just flashed.

The moon shining bright on the midnight dew grass,
Gave luster of feeding as if the gator would pass.

When what to the cats' wondering eyes should appear,
But a miniature sleigh and eight giant reindeer,
With a little old driver so lively and real.
In a moment they thought "a Christmas, eight-deer meal!"

How excited they were, the cats acting tame,
They roared, chuffed, and growled each one the same.
Come to Ula, no, to Pesha, to Lester, to Max,
Those deer look tasty, just look at those racks!

But they didn't land here, for Santa gave a whistle.
They went away from the center like down of a thistle.
But they heard him exclaim as he made them a deal,
"Merry Christmas to all, and tomorrow a huge meal!"

Thursday, January 1

. . . a big cat new year . . .

And so the new year has "roared" in with the cats! I suppose they all stayed up until midnight anticipating the ball drop in New York City and, of course . . . of course, went wild when 2009 had finally arrived!

Thus far, the new year looks to be a good one. The cooler is extremely full, seeing that we received over thirty large animals in the past week . . . the big cats will be eating well again!

We have had a food shortage, which I have been told is weird for this time of year, plus the pneumonia pandemic should literally be sending livestock to the center in herds. The weather has been very warm, then the temperature drops with rain and is followed by sun. Just bizarre. However, the animals have stampeded to our door the past week, filling the cooler and the bellies of the 191 big cats at the center.

Saturday, January 10

. . . squish . . .

Can you imagine an intestinal backup so compacted that surgery would potentially pull out over ten pounds of straw, fur, and food waste? Well, believe me it happens. Perhaps not to humans, but to a cat . . . why not?!

Tish had lived at the rescue center since 2000, when she came from an extreme situation in Pennsylvania of abuse, malnutrition, and unbearable conditions living among feces and rotting meat. She and her cage mate, Goldie, fit in well at the center, with similar stories to many of the cats housed here.

Unfortunately Goldie passed a few years back, before my time at the rescue center, but Tish was still there when I arrived. Basking in the sun on the top level of her climbing tower, eyes closed and a small bit of her tongue sticking out the front of her mouth, she looked down at passersby as if she were a statue of noble grace and beauty. Of course she was all of that. She would often lie along the fence side waiting for keepers to come by and rub her side while she most appreciatively "ohmed" with thanks. ("Ohming" is a friendly lion noise . . . sounds like . . . ooohhhmmm . . .)

This past summer, Tish was no longer excreting waste. Keepers would scour the grounds in hunt of even the smallest fecal sample hidden within the long summer grasses. However, it was never found and her appetite soon ceased as well. She was taken in for an ultrasound and it was found that she had a massive backup in her intestines.

During surgery, over ten pounds of feces, straw, and fur were pulled from within her. It was also most obvious that she was suffering from pancreatic cancer . . . in humans a very fatal type of cancer leaving only but weeks to live. The pancreas controls enzyme function in the small intestine, helping to break down proteins, fats, and carbs. With little to no pancreatic function, Tish was unable to break down her meals, which severely clogged her up.

However, Tish came out of surgery in remarkable shape. Returned to normal conditions: eating, drinking, and excreting waste. She ran around her enclosure, played on her tower, and waited for the keeper scratches through the fence. We still hunted for her feces, and normally one (very large) pile was found daily . . . no worries. She soon got the nickname "Squish" from being so compacted with squishy material.

In late December we had a harder time finding her feces . . . when we did they once again had straw and lots of fur in it. We started finding random piles of vomit as well and worried Tish had fallen back into her summer ways . . . compacted because of low pancreatic function. She would take her food, but the next day we would pull it out of her house untouched. We knew with her age (approx. fifteen) she would not be able to undergo another surgery, nor would it be fair to keep her alive knowing her pancreas was slowly shutting down.

She ended up not interested in food and quit drinking water. She stayed in her box most of the day, seldom coming out. She would "ohm" when we called her name, just to let us know she was there, but the rubs were not as important as they once were. Vomiting was a daily routine.

Unfortunately, this past Wednesday we had to put Tish down. Although that was sad, her life lived at the rescue center was nothing short of fabulous, relaxing, and loving. A necropsy (autopsy for animals) will be performed to see the cause of death, although we expect nothing less than failure of her pancreas and another backup just like the one this summer. She will be cremated, her ashes returning to the center just like those of every cat before her. Like it says on the website, the rescue center provides permanent homes for big cats.

Wednesday, January 14

. . . and now your local on the 8s . . .

Beep beep beep: my alarm rings waking me from the deep depths of my dreams. Can I add what a treacherous sound that is to hear in the morning? I've actually changed to an alarm song, but anyways that doesn't matter.

I hit snooze, just as I do every other morning, and continue this snooze routine for another twenty minutes. I get up, make my oatmeal, and turn on channel 38.

Ooooo, seriously I am excited for the voice, I know it's coming . . . YES! "And now your local on the 8s."

For all you who do not know, the Weather Channel plays local weather on every 8 of the hour . . . say, 2:08 PM, 2:18, 28, 38, so on. This has become a part of my morning I regret missing. See, when you work outside eight to ten hours a day, weather is what you know, very important, highlights of conversation, your life . . . just something you DO NOT miss!

Most of what they say sounds like Charlie Brown's mom from the Peanuts. "Wwaat waat wat wat." I just gaze at the screen and mostly watch numbers that flash up and the radar slowly moving across southern Indiana. Well, this morning, let's say I almost choked.

"Waat waattt minus-eleven degrees, high of two, wind chill minus twenty waat waattt." I thought they were joking, perhaps a crude joke someone was playing to wake me out of my seven-hour slumber/coma. Well, it was no joke, the first step I took towards my car told me just that when my nostrils froze to my inner nose.

At work we do like cold weather. As I have said before, the cold bring cattle stampeding to the door, not alive of course, but hey!! We need the food! Today we only worked half the day, making sure to cover our whole body except a sliver of our eyes to see what we were doing. We went inside every half hour to avoid frostbite and made sure we kept moving swiftly, briskly. Adding to this chill, we had four inches of snow! It was the most snow we have had all winter. Being the Midwesterner I am, I loved the snow. Just like the tigers I was excited for the white fluff, something I've missed all winter. The cats, minus the tigers, stayed in their boxes and seldom came out to purr, ohm, or say hello. We didn't clean or pull bones like usual in any of the cages, the temperatures being too dangerous, even if you are used to cold weather.

Later in the week we would have work to catch up on, once the cold spree moved through. Let's just say, that Friday when it was thirty degrees . . . we cleaned. Do your math . . . if you have six tigers in an enclosure, each going to the bathroom one to two times a day, and we couldn't clean for five days . . . well, that is around thirty to forty large (very large) piles of poo, and that is just one cage. With 191 cats . . . today is going to be a long day.

Wednesday, January 28

. . . a grumbly, rumbly, roaring stomach . . .

Food. Probably one of the dirtiest parts of working at the EFRC. Yes, you can scoop poo, pick up maggot filled bones, even fall prey to the occasional spray, but feeding is where most of the dirty work comes in.

Blood, guts, bones, and internal fluids can get messy, not to mention a bit smelly. I have learned not to take my clothes home with me. They stink, they are always wet with blood, rain, or snow, and frankly they are just too disgusting to deal with unless you plan an immediate laundry date.

So, butchering. Do you ever wonder how it's done? What we use? How we section the animals into meals reasonable for every cat in the center? If so, and if your stomach can handle it, go on and read ahead!

For the most part we feed out cow, horse, deer, or goat, but some cats eat only chicken, which is processed, much the way we see it when we buy raw chicken from the store. The others we butcher in our new building. Cows and horses normally come already deceased. Every once and a while they come alive, and Bill, who drives to get most of our deceased livestock, will put them down humanely.

When we get them we move them into the barn and pull a metal rope around the back hoof of the animal. Typically the head comes off first since the animal can drain most of its blood once it's gone. After the head, we cut off the back leg that is strung in the wire rope. The tension of the animal's weight hanging allows a very clean and fast cut when detaching the leg from the animal. We then take excess meat off the leg, cutting it down to a size that we can carry, and save the chunks. Next is a front leg. We cut it the same as the back, except we leave the shoulder blade attached as well. We take the second front leg next and lastly pull the animal up by the last back leg. We do not take the leg off; instead we cut the chest cavity open and allow the guts (intestines, liver, heart, lungs, etc) to drop into the bucket of the Bobcat. We then take the guts to the compost where they decompose with the help of high temperatures and plenty of bacteria. Since the leg is still attached, we use this time to cut the ribs from the spine, the spine from the brisket, the brisket from the pelvic portion of the animal, and the pelvis from the last remaining leg. Once again, the tension of the animal upside down allows fast and easy cuts. Butchering can take anywhere from twenty to sixty minutes for one animal.

The meat, whether on bone or in chunk, is taken into the cooler (approx. thirty by thirty ft.) where it waits to be fed out to the cats. We feed out approximately three thousand pounds of meat a day—an equivalent of two to four large animals. The meat in the cooler may be fed out immediately or up to a week later.

Front legs will typically be fed to one large cat (lion/tiger), back legs to two cats, along with a chunk, and heads/pelvic/brisket to large groups, with chunks for each additional cat. Ribs will be fed at random. Smaller cats eat chicken, small legs (calf/goat), or small chunks.

Some cats are fed only chicken. Unlike cow or horse, which is red, chicken is white meat and has been found to slow the rate of renal failure in cats. We have many old cats and a few with diagnosed renal failure, and they eat only chicken. Others have allergies to red meat and can only eat white.

All in all, the butchering is well worth the smell, the dirt, the blood, and the grime. The cats need to eat. At the end of the day, looking back at what you have done, accomplished, and achieved, snow, rain, cold, or heat is nothing in the face of the gratification of happy cats.

Thursday, January 29

. . . a day to play in the snow . . .

Let's just say that all cats are not the same when it comes to the enjoyment and the thrill of . . . the excitement about . . . a good January snow. The tigers LOVE the snow. It seems they just cannot get enough of it, running spastically around and chasing each other, only to plow into the fluffy snow-covered ground.

I was so excited a few weeks back when we got an overnight 4 inches . . . WOW was I shocked this past week with the sight I saw Wednesday morning. The weather had said all week that we were supposed to be getting a snowstorm and that it was to be rather large. Tuesday it snowed around 4 inches, continuing with another inch of ice midafternoon and even into the evening when I went to bed. When I awoke the next morning I was shocked by the 12.9 inches that coated the ground, pathway, road, and was still blurring the air and sky outside the window. It was total silence outside; you would have thought Indiana had NEVER seen snow.

Back to the cats! Like I previously stated, the tigers love the snow. I would have to say that they are the only ones in the whole center. The lions trailed minimal paths that were followed throughout the day and even a week later are still the only prints in the cage. If they meet head-to-head, one will back up until one has enough room to pass on the path. Even the cougars that live in the snow don't come out! I plowed a path for Autumn, a cougar, so she would come out of her box! Leopards are the same when it comes to the snow; I think we may have entered every enclosure just to plow a path through to the beast beneath!

Friday, January 30

. . . only to live like royalty . . .

Every cat at the rescue center is special. They are treated with care, with even greater care than many domestic house pets. Whatever they need it is there immediately, whether medication or surgery or basics such as food or straw.

Many of our cats take medication like vitamins daily, primarily for everyday health, but many of them have also aged to the point where other medication is now just as important as an everyday meal. Prince was one of those cats.

Rescued from a circus in Peru, Indiana, Prince was one of nine tigers brought to the rescue center with memories of homes as small as that of a large dog kennel and had abilities that went beyond roaring. Several of these cats came able to stand atop a telephone pole, on all four paws. Others were able to stand on their back two legs and walk in a circle. Cool to think about, but very sad when you realize the conditions the cats who had these talents lived under. Could you imagine never being able to run? To stretch out? Barely even walk? When cats live in a circus cage and are only exercised for money and a cheering crowd, not only are the people at risk of the animals becoming aggressive from being caged, but also the cats' lives are in danger if they do turn on the crowd or their trainers. The circus is a dangerous life and definitely not one fit for tigers, who are undernourished and poorly cared for.

Prince and Princess lived together on the west side of the center, spending most of their days wallowing in a water tub, climbing a three-tier tower, and lying in a box. No worries, screaming crowds, or small cages.

Cats have weird ways of passing on, many times disappearing to die alone or even hopping to a favorite place they haven't been able to reach for years. Last March Princess climbed the tower she hadn't conquered in years. Seeing that she was eighteen years old, it was odd she pulled a stunt like this. As she reached the top, she had a stroke and passed away. Since her death Prince has never been the same.

They say that love separation is many times the hardest on animals, and the stress of being alone will depress them to the point where they eventually pass as well. Prince was a prime example. He no longer went into the box he once loved. He paced by day, and from what we could tell never, NEVER stopped walking. In all twenty years of life, Prince constantly walked.

In the past months Prince's health has steadily declined, his back legs unable to support his weight. We placed him on strong doses of pred-nisone, an immunosuppressant that affects the immune system, many times used for kidney disease, inflammation, and autoimmune diseases . . . essentially a steroid. Just as with pets at home, in the later years of their life you take into special consideration their pain, even the quality of life. The prednisone kept Prince walking (something he never stopped) and on his feet. The stagger he once had had ceased, his back legs began supporting him again. When you take medications so often, they start to lose their kick, and as with humans, Prince also had to take larger doses to keep him comfortable. His walk became a limp, the limp a stagger, and the stagger soon became a swagger to the point where walking a straight line was hard for him to do without dropping to the ground at least once.

Unlike Tish, Prince had no trouble eating, and since he was taking a steroid, eating was something he loved to do most. He also continued regular excretion function.

Friday, Prince's health was failing fast, and so was his back end. The spirit and life in his eyes had gone and his expressions were gray. He wasn't interested in his medication anymore and even struggled to visit us at the fence, something he usually enjoyed doing. That afternoon we found Prince in Princess's side of the box, where he hadn't gone in over a year. Motionless. Fred had already come to put him down; however, we feel Prince had the same idea. We poked his back side with a stick, hoping to rouse him from the box. Motionless. We saw him breathing, but no jump or reaction. We did tranquilize him just out of precaution; there was no flinch, no movement, he just stayed still. He was ready.

It is always hard to put an animal down, but I believe it is harder to watch them suffer. At the end of their life you have to consider their comfort and the quality of life they are living, even if it does mean you have to assist them to the light.

Saturday, February 7

. . . an aggressive attempt for food . . .

We are taught when we are young to always share with our neighbor,

G. G., November 29, 2008 (above), and King, October 5, 2008 (below)

whether it is the kid sitting next to us or the person next door in need of a cup of sugar. We understand these concepts and eventually it just becomes part of our nature . . . to lend that helping hand. However, these ideas are not instilled in wild animals and by saying "not," I mean sharing is something unheard of. The cats are greedy. Have you ever watched dogs share their bowl of food? Or even give their favorite bone to the pup next to them just to be nice? No, and big cats are not much different except for the size of the bite behind the growl and the animal behind the guarded object.

Food is one of the main things they will guard. Many of them do not like to share food or even be approached when food is in sight. That is why I took advantage of the very angry lion, King, at feeding time. He is actually so food aggressive that his two cage mates, Jasmine and Lauren, have to be locked in the small part so he will not tear after them in a frantic panic assuming they will steal his food!

It is a daily routine. We drive down in our foodmobile, stop at the end of his enclosure, lock the girls in while he sits in the corner and grumbles like a Harley-Davidson traveling at a low speed. Once we give him his food he is fine, but until then . . . WATCH OUT!

Audra calming Bob, July 19, 2009

Frequently Asked Questions

New visitors to EFRC ask lots of questions. Here is EFRC's Frequently Asked Questions list:

Where do the cats come from?

The abused, neglected, and abandoned felines have been confiscated from illegal owners or arrive from circuses, substandard zoos, and other facilities that have been closed for a variety of reasons.

Who names the cats?

If a cat arrives with a name, the cat will keep that name. If a cat arrives nameless, one can donate $500 to name the cat. Otherwise, staff will choose a name.

Why are some cats alone, while others are in groups?

If cats arrive together, the Center houses them together unless hostilities arise. As a rule, newly arrived older felines remain by themselves because of the difficulty of introducing older felines to unfamiliar felines unless both cats lived with other cats in the past. If a single cat arrives before its first birthday, attempts will be made to introduce it to another young feline.

How long do the cats live?

In the wild, the big cats live seven to ten years. In captivity, it is possible for a big cat to live into their late teens or early twenties. Our oldest cat, Kashka (a female tiger), lived to be twenty-three years old.

How much do the cats weigh?

At birth, lions and tigers weigh 2–3 pounds. Adult male lions can weigh up to 500 pounds, while adult tigers can weigh up to and over 700 pounds. Most full-grown leopards and cougars weigh between 80–150 pounds; the smaller felines weigh up to 60 pounds.

Do you have Siberian or Bengal tigers?

The Center assumes that most of the tigers are mixes of Bengal and Amur (Siberian) subspecies. Owing to inappropriate breeding practices, the cats do not arrive with papers.

Are the cats permitted to go outside of their enclosures to exercise?

No. We provide large and enriched natural habitats.

Does anyone go into the cats' enclosures?

When needed, the director, assistant director, and head keeper enter the enclosures of a select few cats. Other members of the staff are permitted protected contact with some of the felines.

Which cats roar?

Lions, tigers, and leopards roar, while cougars, bobcats, and servals purr.

What is a friendly cat sound?

Tigers will greet people and each other with chuffing.

Do they eat every day?

Servals, ocelots, and bobcats eat daily. Lions, tigers, and cougars fast one day a week in the winter and two days a week in the heat of the summer. In the wild none of these animals eat every day.

Where does the meat come from?

When one of their cows, calves, or horses dies, farmers contact the Center. A staff member travels to the farm, loads the deceased animal, and brings it back to the Center where it is processed. The Center also receives roadkill deer and purchases poultry.

How much meat does the Center use daily?

The Center uses three thousand pounds of food seven days a week.

Why do the cats spray?

The cats spray to mark their territory.

Are bobcats as sweet as they look?

No! Furthermore, they are extremely private animals.

Do the cats respond to "Here, kitty, kitty"?

No, but most do respond to their names if in the mood.

Does the Center have a veterinarian on staff?

Dr. Fred Froderman, DVM, from Clear Lake Veterinary Hospital takes care of the big cats at the on-site clinic. If a medical need cannot be addressed in the Center's clinic, the cat is transported to the University of Illinois–Champaign/Urbana. The veterinarians from the university can perform certain procedures at the on-site clinic as well.

Do the veterinarians donate their services?

No, but the Center does receive a discount.

Does the Center sell cats to zoos?

No. If a cat comes to the Center, it will stay at the Center for its lifetime.

What happens to the cats when they die?

A necropsy is performed to determine the cause of death. Afterward, the cat is cremated, and its ashes are kept at the Center.

How many employees does the Center have?

The Center has approximately twelve employees. The keepers are college graduates holding degrees in zoology, biology, or animal behavior. College interns and volunteers also work at the Center.

How can I volunteer at the Center?

The first requirement is to visit EFRC. If you are interested in volunteering, contact the assistant director and commit to volunteer twice a month (four to six hours each visit). All volunteers must be at least eighteen years old.

How can the general public help exotic felines?

There are several ways for people to help exotic felines and ease their plight. Never attend or participate in events that exploit animals (don't go to circuses, don't patronize photo booths incorporating big cats, don't pay for the opportunity to touch a big cat, don't visit substandard zoos). Never buy an exotic cat, because they are not suitable as pets. Take the time to learn about big cats, their habitats, and efforts to help save them. Take the time to learn about all endangered animals. Donate money to your favorite animal charity. (Do research to ensure that money is indeed going to animal care.) Educate your friends and family regarding big cats and their needs.

First-time visitors can contact EFRC at:

Exotic Feline Rescue Center
2221 E. Ashboro Road
Center Point, IN 47840
812-835-1130
e-mail: efrc1@verizon.net

For more information, visit the Center's website:
http://www.exoticfelinerescuecenter.org/

Office, motel, operating room,
August 11, 2004

Melanie Bowlin has been a teacher of Deaf and Hard-of-Hearing children for twenty-one years and is currently employed by the Metropolitan School District of Wayne Township in Indianapolis. Her free time is spent giving tours at EFRC.

Audra Masternak graduated from Albion College in 2008 and interned at EFRC. While at the Center she kept a blog documenting her daily routine.

Stephen D. McCloud has been a passionate photographer since his teen years. For the past thirty years, he has worked in the Information Technology Department at Indiana State University. McCloud's portfolio includes sports photography, natural landscapes, oddities, and exotic felines. He is a regular volunteer at EFRC.